PRIORITY TIME
Addicted to God's Word

Daily + Unhurried + Inspired

CHRIS CONLEE

CONTENTS

FOREWORD

Welcome! Let me introduce you to a new term: Priority Time. It's the one priority that will determine all other priorities! I am privileged to invite you into this study created by my friend and partner in ministry, Chris Conlee. One of the great privileges of my life has been working alongside Chris to plant and lead Highpoint Church in Memphis, TN, where Chris has served as the lead pastor since the church started in 2002. In order to understand this study, you need to know the author.

The only word that adequately describes Chris is "relentless." Chris has the mental tenacity of a drill sergeant, yet he is kind, compassionate and deeply committed to Jesus Christ. After spending more than a decade in close quarters with Chris, I have seen the good, the bad and the ugly (just as he has of me). I believe a man's character is not found in his successful moments but rather in how he handles failure and struggle. I have seen Chris at his best and at his worst, and Chris is truly a man of godly character. This is why the word "relentless" fits Chris so well. He relentlessly loves and serves his wife Karin and his children, Mark and Annika. He relentlessly cares for and loves people after others have forgotten. He relentlessly seeks to learn and grow, and he never accepts the status quo. He relentlessly pushes Highpoint Church to maximize its potential with challenging messages and inspiring vision. Above all, he is relentless in his pursuit of God's Word. His determination and discipline to spend time in God's Word and prayer each day defines Chris as a spiritual leader worth following. The mark of a good pastor is not found in his résumé, his speaking ability, the number of books on his bookshelf, the size of the building he preaches in or the Sunday attendance – it is found in knowing confidently that this man walks with God. Chris walks with God. The book you are holding is the result of Chris's relentless, daily pursuit of God's truth.

This study is designed to replicate a relentless spirit in you to pursue God through the bible and prayer. A daily priority time is intended to be more than a devotional – it is intended to be transformational. It seems every good church member out there has a quiet time, which begs the question, "Where are the results?" Even the words "quiet time" communicate something different from what God intends to accomplish in our time with Him. God still speaks. His Word is still living and active. He still seeks to transform lives! Our daily time with Him should not be defined by the word "quiet." I love the phrase "priority time" that Chris introduces in this study. Doesn't that sound better to you? We must prioritize our time with Him and prioritize obedience to the truth we discover.

I pray that you will be as blessed by this resource as I have been. The insights and steps Chris presents here are time-tested and life-changing. This journey will require desire, discipline and determination. It will not be easy, but let's face it, the things we value most in life are rarely easy. In Paul's letter to Timothy we are told, *"[F]or while bodily training is of some value, godliness is of value in every way, as it holds promise for the present life and also for the life to come"* (1 Timothy 4:8 ESV). I urge you to make the most of this study. You are holding a unique opportunity to take your own walk with God to the next level. I hope you will pray as Chris has prayed so many times, "God, show me Your glory," as you begin the addiction of a daily priority time.

Your fellow addict,

Andy Savage

Teaching Pastor, Highpoint Church
highpointmemphis.com | andysavage.com | @andysavage

Part One
MY ADDICTION

Chapter 1:
Addicted to the World

My name is Chris Conlee, and I am a follower of Jesus Christ who struggles with the flesh. For the first twenty-six years of my life, I was addicted to the lust of the flesh, the lust of the eyes, and the boastful pride of life. I was compulsively devoted to loving myself, money and pleasure. All of us are addicted to our sins of choice, but few of us are willing to admit it. The first step to overcoming an addiction is to come out of denial and admit the problem. Step 1 of *Celebrate Recovery* reads, "We admitted we are powerless over our addictions and compulsive behaviors, that our lives had become unmanageable."[1]

This is my story of old addictions and new addictions. It is my story of trying to take off the old and put on the new. It is the private battle of Romans 7:14-25 that none of us wants to admit publicly. Can you identify with Romans 7:19: *"For the good that I want, I do not do, but I practice the very evil that I do not want"*?

I'd grown skeptical and cynical of recovery programs, churches, conferences and counseling that promised life change. I learned the hard way that self-help doesn't work. I was not good at helping myself. I was tired of trying and failing and hitting the bottom only to find out there is a deeper bottom. If I've learned anything about my addiction to the flesh, it's that I can't overcome my addiction through more education, discipline or motivation.

How did I overcome my addiction to sin? How can you overcome your addiction to sin? The only way to overcome an addiction is to replace it with one that is greater. I must replace my *addiction to the world* with an *addiction to the Word*. I must replace my addiction to sin with an addiction to God. My story of recovery isn't the story of recovery. It is the story of a greater addiction.

Are you struggling with the "addicted" terminology? Some of you are thinking, "'Addicted' is such a strong word. I make mistakes and bad choices occasionally, but I'm not addicted to sin. I know I'm not perfect, but I believe I'm a good person." I'm not saying you're a bad person if you are addicted to sin. You are a normal person who needs to normalize the problem of sin in order to overcome your sin.

You must see your sin from God's perspective before you can understand the true danger of it. Denial never leads to recovery. The more you deny your sin, the more you live in it, but the more you confess your sin, the more you overcome it. Apart from the Word of God, I didn't improve with time, and I didn't outgrow my problems. Sin doesn't naturally become less tempting. Ignoring sin always leads to more sin in my life. Whatever goes unmanaged in my life becomes unmanageable.

Are you justifying your goodness or are you desperate to overcome your addiction to sin? Are you afraid of your sins or do you think you can manage your sins? Let me share with you a common denominator among godly men and women: The closer they get to God, the more they confess their sinfulness.

Why is that? The more you see His holiness, the more you see your lack of holiness. The more you see that He is the "Great I Am," the more you realize that you are the "Great I Am Not." Holiness isn't determined by the *absence* of sin; it is determined by your *response* to sin.

The longer I live and serve as a pastor, the more the urgency of this book burns within me because I'm tired of watching Christians live defeated lives. It frustrates me to watch believers be controlled by lesser addictions. What if there was a greater desire than our selfish ones? What if there was a greater love than our love of self, money and pleasure? What if there was a new addiction – a greater addiction?

I can guarantee results from this book because what I'm about to teach you changes my life daily and has changed the lives of men and women throughout history. The words and ideas that fill the following pages are not untested, abstract concepts to me; they are the story of a greater addiction. Before I go any further, let me begin by telling you my story.

I grew up in a typical, middle-class, hard-working, well-intentioned, imperfect family. We were "Christians" – the Christmas and Easter kind. We were church members and we were baptized, but we weren't different from non-Christians. We knew we should be holy (radically different, unique and set apart from the world's ways). We were convicted that we should be different. We even wanted to be different, but we weren't. We wanted to change, but we couldn't. We knew we should die to the flesh, but we were still addicted to it.

Occasionally, we would get motivated to change and

would go to church for weeks in a row. Attendance would eventually wane, and we would turn back to living the lie of sin management that says you can control sin. The truth is sin controls you. If no one sees you sin, you think you've gotten away with it. If you don't suffer consequences immediately, you think you've safely managed your sin. We weren't good at sin management or attendance, so we gave up on both and went back to playing golf on Sundays. I wasn't a good Christian, but I was becoming a great golfer!

When I was fifteen, I went to a youth camp in Destin, FL, where I trusted Christ as my Lord and Savior. Salvation was definitely the first step to change. But my addiction to God was inconsistent, and my addiction to sin was consistent. I was *forgiven* immediately for my sin, but I wasn't immediately *freed* from it. I thought everything would change instantly, almost magically. I hadn't learned the principle of sowing and reaping. I didn't know how to grow or walk in Christ. I wasn't even good at attending church, but that was the only thing I knew for certain I was supposed to do.

That fall, I went to a private Christian school. My attendance patterns definitely improved between school-required chapel and girlfriend-inspired church attendance. What was the end result of my improved attendance? Was I growing in faith, hope and love? Was I changing? I didn't cuss or drink as much, and I tried not to cross the purity line in dating. Have you ever asked the question, "How close to sin can I get without sinning?" Looking back, I see that was the deception and manipulation of the Liar. The goal of my hormone-driven teenage years was to figure out how to sin without technically sinning.

During high school and the first three years of college, I defined success as a Christian by the things I said "no" to instead of the things I said "yes" to. I didn't have a vision for who God wanted me to be; I just knew who I wasn't supposed to be.

I defined life change by the word "don't" instead of the word "do." My understanding of Christianity was, "Don't think that or say that and definitely don't do that!" You will never overcome an addiction by saying, "Don't." I knew I wasn't supposed to be addicted to sex, drugs and rock 'n' roll, but I had no idea what I *was* supposed to be addicted to as a man of God.

I was not prepared for the choices and challenges of college. The first time I walked into my dorm room, four or five guys looked at me and said, "Hey, rookie, go get us some more beer." Church attendance never prepared me for this moment because I wasn't prepared for real life. I knew right from wrong, but my desire to be *liked* was stronger than my desire to do *right*. I spent the next three years *addicted to the world* instead of *addicted to the Word*.

Chapter 2:
Addicted to the Word

During my junior year at the University of Memphis, I walked into a Fellowship of Christian Athletes (FCA) meeting for the first time and somehow walked out as the vice president. I guess the qualifications were private Christian high school and Christmas/ Easter church attendance! In hindsight it seems comical, but God used that experience in my life. That night began my search for something more – a new, pure and stronger addiction. I knew I didn't want to be a hypocrite, but I didn't know what I wanted to be. I didn't know what a godly man looked like or did. All I knew was that a godly man was supposed to go to church, be a good family man and be successful in his career.

At this point I had been a Christian for six years, but I had never read my bible. I had heard the bible taught, but I had never read one book of the bible from beginning to end. During my freshman year in high school, I made a 46 in my first bible class. I regret saying this, but I learned how to cheat my way through bible classes. I had attended church, chapel and bible classes, but I had never picked up the bible and read the Sermon on the Mount, much less the gospel of Matthew. What changed when I became vice president of the FCA? I picked up a workbook called *Experiencing God: Knowing and Doing the Will of God* by Henry Blackaby, Richard Blackaby and Claude King. God used this study to get me into scripture for the first time in my life. I did the study three times that year. Strangely, it was almost like an addiction.

I went from Christmas and Easter attendance to spending five days a week with God in His Word. God used this study to give me a vision for life that far exceeded the word "don't." I finally had a vision that was bigger than church attendance, bigger than being a family man and bigger than having a successful career. I had a vision for knowing and doing the will of God. I was beginning to *"taste and see that the Lord is good"* (Psalm 34:8). I was experimenting with a new and pure addiction.

I developed a vision to know Christ and to make Him known. I didn't own the vision; it owned me. I still don't fully understand it all, but I met "The Great I Am" (Exodus 3:14). I asked to see the glory of God, and He entered my dorm room and proclaimed,

"The LORD, the LORD God, compassionate and gracious, slow to anger, and abounding in loving kindness and truth" (Exodus 34:6). Every lesser desire and dream died that semester. I died to my lifelong dream of playing professional golf and pursued the vision of loving God, loving people and making disciples.

I experienced my first season of sustained life change through *Experiencing God* and my time in the bible. This season of life change lasted two years, and immediately after graduation it unpredictably sent me to seminary where I anticipated an incredible time of spiritual growth. I attended bible classes four days a week, chapel four days a week and church multiple times a week. I read books about God, books about the bible and even memorized scripture, but something was missing. I finished my first year of seminary, but my spiritual growth didn't match the growth I had when I was studying *Experiencing God*.

What was missing? I attended and read everything, but I was failing to overcome my addiction to sin again. I asked my friends about their walks with God and learned that they, too, were struggling. How could this be? I wasn't *growing spiritually*; I was just becoming *more educated*.

The summer after my first year of seminary, I met a man named Clyde Cranford, and everything changed.

Clyde mentored me and taught me how to read the bible in such a way that I would know the God of the bible, not just the bible. This was radically different from my previous experiences. This was a new addiction. An *addiction to the Word* always overcomes an *addiction to the world*.

When Clyde read the bible, he knew the author of the bible. When he read the bible, he wasn't reading black ink on white pages – he was sitting across from God and having a conversation with Him. He was in the very presence of God, and he was hearing the Word of God spoken directly to him through the illumination of the Holy Spirit. When Clyde read scripture, I fell in love with his God. I couldn't get enough.

Clyde taught me to read scripture as a person in the story. I became an actor who read the script from the perspective of each character. Clyde taught me how to hear the voice of God specifically and directly, and how to *"be still, and know that [He is] God"* (Psalm 46:10 ESV). He taught me how to be like Mary who sat at the feet of Jesus and gazed at His face. I learned that prayer wasn't talking as much as it was listening. He taught me to listen and to obey. He gave me a taste of the Word of God, and my appetite increased.

The importance of these truths took on new meaning after I became a dad. I remember waking up one morning when Mark, my son, was about eighteen months old. I heard him in his crib saying, "Da Da." When I opened the door, he stretched his arms wide open, looked me in the eyes and said, "Da Da." I picked him up, and he embraced me. I immediately sensed God saying to me, "That's the way I want you to greet me every morning!"

God used Clyde to teach me how to meet with my Father every morning. That is the greatest gift anyone has ever given me. It is also the gift I want to give you through this book. The passion of my life is for you to read the *Word of God* to know the *God of the Word*. This is the greater addiction because an addiction to God always overcomes an addiction to sin.

For the next three years, I spent every Friday afternoon with Clyde. I'd sit down, and he would ask me, "What did God say to you this week?" He didn't ask how many times I had a priority time that week. Addicts don't have to be asked if they used last week. Of course they used; they're addicts. They are compulsively devoted to a habit-forming substance. It was Clyde's goal for me to be compulsively devoted to the habit-forming substance of the Word of God. In this analogy of addictions, Clyde didn't ask me if I used; he asked me about the high. He didn't ask me how many times I had a priority time that week; he asked me what God said to me through my time in the Word and prayer. He asked what I learned about the character of God and about my character. He always wanted to know what God said to me in prayer and not what I asked from God. He wanted to know if I was listening and responding to God. He was interested in my love for God.

One Friday afternoon we had together was a defining moment in my life. Clyde asked, "What did God say to you this week?" I was excited to share with Clyde because I had a powerful encounter with God during my priority time. I told him God showed me that I wanted to be super, great and fantastic but for all the *wrong* reasons and that I needed to be super, great and fantastic for all the *right* reasons. I was really proud of myself and thought Clyde would be really proud of me, too.

Clyde looked me in the eyes and asked, "Chris, you know that I love you, don't you?" I replied, "Yes." He said, "Chris, the bible never tells you to be super, great and fantastic; it tells you to deny yourself daily, pick up your cross and follow Him." He continued, "There is only One who is super, great and fantastic, and it isn't you." The Holy Spirit crushed me in that moment. Spiritually, I hit bottom that day. I literally wept with the same intensity as when my brother was killed in a car/train wreck when I was ten. I wept that way because I died that day. Death is always painful and always requires grieving. Clyde hugged me while I wept, and after thirty minutes he looked at me and said, "I love you. Let's go to a movie."

What did Clyde teach me? He taught me how to meditate on scripture. To meditate is to focus my thinking on the God of the Word. When you focus your thinking, when you apply God's truth and interact with God in prayer, God teaches you how to die, live and love. The Holy Spirit leads you to confess, repent and believe. God uses my priority time to teach me to be holy: to be radically different and set apart; "YOU SHALL BE HOLY, FOR I AM HOLY" (1 Peter 1:16).

What is my secret to life change? It is my priority of putting God first. It is the one priority that determines all my priorities and protects me from self destruction. It is the one priority that makes me less like Chris and more like Christ. It is my daily dating relationship with the One whom I love with all my heart, soul, mind and strength.

A priority time isn't my spiritual *discipline*; it is my spiritual *addiction*. I have an addictive personality. If I'm not addicted to God, then I'm addicted to myself. I'm addicted to "*the lust of the flesh and the lust of the eyes and the boastful pride of life*" (1 John 2:16-17). Apart from the work of the Holy Spirit in my life, I'm addicted to being a lover of self, money and pleasure rather than a lover of God (2 Timothy 3:1-5).

Pause for a minute and try to comprehend the tragedy of being addicted to sin. The greatest tragedy isn't the consequence of disobedience; it is never knowing the results of obedience. It is never knowing the joy of worshiping, loving and serving God. It is never knowing the joy of loving and serving others. My addiction to sin is an addiction to myself. It is a deliberate choice to put myself first and everyone else a distant second.

An addict is one who is compulsively devoted to a habit-forming substance, and my substance of choice is the Word of

God. I'm either addicted to the *world* or to the *Word*. My heart is never in neutral. It is either compulsively devoted to myself or to God.

My priority time helps me overcome my addiction to the flesh. It replaces impure addictions with pure addictions and impure pleasures with pure pleasures. It enables me to renew my mind, heart and desires with the habit-forming substance of the Word.

The Liar has convinced us that God is boring and that God's Word is about rules instead of a relationship. Can you name one boring addiction? No one is addicted to boring drugs, and no one is addicted to a boring God. We must learn that the only way to triumph over sin is to find superior satisfaction in God.

All addictions begin with an encounter, and my addiction to God's Word began when I experienced Clyde's relationship with God. Addictions are never based on *information*; addictions are always *experiential*. We need to drink deeply from the Word of God. We need to *"taste and see that the LORD is good"* (Psalm 34:8). There is a radical difference between *reading* the Word of God and being *addicted* to the Word of God.

A priority time is the one addiction I will endorse. I am a living testimony to the power of this addiction. I am addicted to reading the *Word of God* to know the *God of the Word*.

Welcome to my recovery group! Whether we realize it or not, we are all recovering from our addiction to sin. My story of recovery isn't the story of recovery; it is the story of a greater addiction. It isn't the story of "Just Say No." It is the story of "Just Say Yes." I am a believer of Jesus Christ who struggles with the flesh, but I'm overcoming impure addictions with pure addictions. That's my story, and I'm confident it can be yours, too.

Are you ready to get high?

Part Two
MY RECOVERY

Chapter 3:
A New Priority

A new addiction is a new priority because you are compulsively devoted to your habit-forming substance. You are addicted to a power greater than yourself whether that is sin or God. If you are *addicted to sin*, it is a power that leads to *insanity*. If you are *addicted to God*, it is a power that leads to *sanity*.

It was through Clyde's life that I experienced the truth of Step 2 of the 12-step process of *Celebrate Recovery*: "We came to believe that a power greater than ourselves could restore us to sanity."[1] Clyde was introducing me to a new addiction, a new power and a new recovery group. My definition of church began to change. It was no longer the place for all the good people; it was a recovery group for people who were breaking their addiction to sin.

The leader of the group was the "Friend of Sinners," and He was offering a new sobriety plan. The people in the group weren't talking about their old addictions; they were talking about a new addiction, a new power that was producing amazing results.

Let me give you an example from one of the people in my recovery group. I received a phone call from a friend. She was fired up and said, "I have to tell somebody about my priority time this morning." Remember, she has a new addiction. She couldn't wait until group time, so she called me as a fellow group member. She told me John 1:29 says, "*The next day [John the Baptist] saw Jesus coming to him and said, 'Behold, the Lamb of God who takes away the sin of the world!'*" She talked for forty-five minutes without taking a breath. She couldn't stop talking about the God who took away her addiction to sin. She was just like Peter and John in Acts 4:20 who said, "*[W]e cannot stop speaking about what we have seen and heard.*" God was replacing her addiction to the world with an addiction to the Word.

She didn't just learn a truth about God; she had an encounter with God. She called with excitement, awe and love in her voice. She didn't just read, apply and pray the Word; she worshiped the God of the Word. She didn't call to tell me a truth about God; she called to tell me about the Lamb of God.

My friend has a priority time because she has a new priority. This daily meeting with God helps her overcome her addiction to sin.

A priority time is a daily, unhurried, inspired time to read the *Word of God* to know the *God of the Word*. It is a commitment to focus your thinking on the Word of God, to personally apply the truths of God, to interact with God in prayer and to document God's activity by writing in a journal. Bottom line, it is all about your relationship with God. It is a daily dating relationship with God.

I must spend time with my wife Karin to build my relationship with her, and there are many ways to accomplish this. We spend time together with our friends and with our kids, and we also work together. We go to the Orpheum Theatre or to Tiger basketball games together. All of that is fun and necessary, but if we don't spend one-on-one time together, something is missing. Nothing replaces one-on-one conversation with Karin. It is the one priority that determines the intimacy of our relationship.

It is exactly the same in my relationship with God. Church attendance is important, but nothing replaces one-on-one conversation with the God of the universe. I need Sunday conversation to enhance and compliment my Monday through Saturday conversations. How healthy would my relationship with Karin be if I only saw her once a week? Similarly, Sunday should be the celebration of my relationship with God, not my attempt to get out of the dog house. It should be my time to worship God, connect with friends and serve according to my strengths.

Busyness is the enemy of intimacy. Therefore, your priority time is the best way to protect and prioritize your relationship with God.

Chapter 4:
A New Pleasure

Why do people use drugs? There are many reasons, but one of them is the promise of a new pleasure. All of us have believed the lies of advertising. People who sell addictions don't sell their products; they sell a lifestyle and an image. We've all heard the saying, "What happens in Vegas, stays in Vegas." You may not have believed the Vegas advertisement, but you've believed many like it. You've believed the advertisements promoting sex, or advertising firms wouldn't use it in virtually every commercial. When you are addicted to sin, you have believed the devil's lie of a new pleasure. The devil's lies always result in "hurts, habits and hang-ups."[1]

How has the church bought the devil's lie of pleasure? The church says, "Sin isn't fun; don't do it." But that simply isn't true and is a bigger lie than the devil's! The church will never help people overcome sin if we can't even admit that sin is fun.

Test question: "Do you *want* to sin?" How did you answer that question? We immediately say "no," but when faced with temptation, we aren't as confident. Let me ask the question again: "Do you *want* to sin?" Honestly, it depends on the sin. Some sins are more tempting to us than other sins. In the moment of temptation, we *want* to sin because the Liar makes sin look attractive. Satan is a professional liar who thrives on deceiving us about pleasure.

How do we overcome our addiction to pleasure? We will never break our addiction to pleasure. The devil didn't create pleasure; he attempts to steal it from God. Every sin is simply the devil taking God's pleasures out of context.

For example, is sex sinful? No. It is pure and beautiful within the covenant of marriage. How do you overcome your desire for sex? You don't because it is a God-given desire. God isn't asking you not to take pleasure in a God-given desire, but He is asking you to do so within the context of *love* instead of *lust*. You must replace impure desires with pure ones. You must want the *intimacy* of sex more than you want the *act* of sex. Pursuing intimacy requires prioritizing the love relationship found in Ephesians 5:25: "*Husbands, love your wives, just as Christ also loved the church and gave Himself up for her."*

We must reclaim God's pleasures. You must fight *worldly pleasure* with *godly pleasure*. God created pleasure and desires to share it with His children. You will never overcome sinful pleasures with a "Just Say No" approach; you overcome sinful pleasures by saying "yes" to God.

Why should you have a priority time? There is no greater pleasure than knowing God and making Him known. It is a pleasure to respond to the love of God with love. It is a pleasure to read the *Word of God* and to know the *God of the Word*. Let me ask the question again: "Why should you have a priority time?" The best answer is because you want to.

If that desire isn't strong enough yet, follow the progression of the arguments in *The Old Addiction* and *The New Addiction* diagram below. Also, use the diagram on the following page to discover *The Glorious Addiction*.

The Old Addiction

Why do you sin?
You don't love God enough.
▼
Why don't you love God enough?
You don't know God.
▼
Why don't you know God?
You don't spend time in God's Word.
▼
Why don't you spend time in God's Word?
You don't see the need.
▼
Why don't you see the need?
Pride.

The New Addiction

It brings glory to God.
What does obeying God do?
▲
It leads you to obey God.
What does loving God do?
▲
It causes you to love God.
What does knowing God do?
▲
It helps you to know God.
What does spending time in God's Word do?
▲
It inspires you to spend time in God's Word.
What does seeing your need do?
▲
It helps you to see your need.
What does humility do?
▲
Humility.
What is the opposite of pride?

The Glorious Addiction

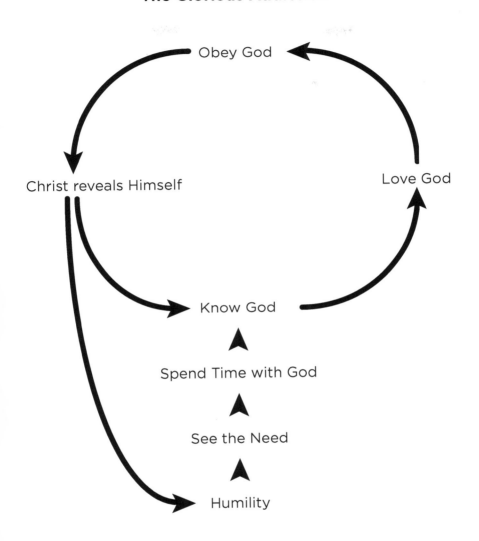

John 14:21
"He who has My commandments and keeps them is the one who loves Me; and he who loves Me will be loved by My Father, and I will love him and will disclose Myself to him."

The following verses speak to the importance and value of renewing your mind with the Word of God. Don't read these passages too quickly because learning to read and apply scripture is the purpose of this book. Some books change your *thinking*, but the bible is the only book that changes your *nature*. The Word of God changes you from the inside out. It changes *whom* you love and *how* you love. It changes your desires as it introduces you to a new priority, a new pleasure and a new purpose.

Psalm 19:7-11
⁷The law of the LORD is perfect, restoring the soul; the testimony of the LORD is sure, making wise the simple. ⁸The precepts of the LORD are right, rejoicing the heart; the commandment of the LORD is pure, enlightening the eyes. ⁹The fear of the LORD is clean, enduring forever; the judgments of the LORD are true; they are righteous altogether. ¹⁰They are more desirable than gold, yes, than much fine gold; sweeter also than honey and the drippings of the honeycomb. ¹¹Moreover, by them Your servant is warned; in keeping them there is great reward.

Psalm 1:2-3
²But his delight is in the law of the LORD, and in His law he meditates day and night. ³He will be like a tree firmly planted by streams of water, which yields its fruit in its season and its leaf does not wither; and in whatever he does, he prospers.

Psalm 119:11
Your word I have treasured in my heart, that I may not sin against You.

Joshua 1:8
This book of the law shall not depart from your mouth, but you shall meditate on it day and night, so that you may be careful to do according to all that is written in it; for then you will make your way prosperous, and then you will have success.

Romans 12:2

And do not be conformed to this world, but be transformed by the renewing of your mind, so that you may prove what the will of God is, that which is good and acceptable and perfect.

2 Timothy 3:14-17

[14]You, however, continue in the things you have learned and become convinced of, knowing from whom you have learned them, [15]and that from childhood you have known the sacred writings which are able to give you the wisdom that leads to salvation through faith which is in Christ Jesus. [16]All scripture is inspired by God and profitable for teaching, for reproof, for correction, for training in righteousness; [17]so that the man of God may be adequate, equipped for every good work.

Are you inspired? Are you motivated? Now, let's learn the purpose of a priority time.

Chapter 5:
A New Purpose

The purpose of a priority time isn't bible study alone; it is *relational intimacy* and *life change*. It is my desire to redefine your understanding of a devotional time or quiet time. Your priority time must be more than reading a page from Oswald Chambers' book, *My Utmost for His Highest*. Long-term, your relationship will not be intimate and your life will not change because of five or ten minute priority times. God must be the focus of your morning so that He can be the focus of your day.

A priority time isn't a spiritual check in the box; it is the beginning of an all-consuming, passionate, relentless pursuit of God. James 4:8 says, *"Draw near to God and He will draw near to you."* One of the keys to a dynamic priority time is high expectations. That's why I pray the prayer of Exodus 33:18 each morning where Moses implores, *"I pray You, show me Your glory!"* I'm expecting so much more than bible study; I'm expecting to see the glory of God.

Before I introduce you to the *Steps to Addiction*, you need to learn three foundational principles of biblical interpretation. In *Living by the Book*, author Howard Hendricks, one of the most respected seminary professors of the last century, defines them this way:

Observation
In this step, you ask and answer the question, "What do I see?" The moment you come to the scriptures you ask, "What are the facts?" You assume the role of a biblical detective, looking for clues. No detail is trivial.

Interpretation
Here you ask and answer the question, "What does it mean?" Your quest is for meaning. Unfortunately, too much bible study begins with interpretation, and furthermore, it usually ends there. Before you understand, you have to learn to see.

Application
Here you ask and answer the question, "How does it work?" not "Does it work?" People say they're going to make the bible relevant. But if the bible is not already relevant, nothing you or I do will help. The bible is relevant because it is revealed. It's always a return to reality. And for those who read it and apply it, it changes their lives.[2]

(If you desire a more comprehensive study of these principles, I recommend the following resources: *Living by the Book* by Howard and William Hendricks; *How to Study your Bible* by Kay Arthur, David Arthur and Pete De Lacy; and *Bible Study Methods* by Rick Warren.)

From these principles, I want to introduce you to the four *Steps to Addiction*:

1. **Focused Thinking:** Addicted to Truth

2. **Personal Application:** Addicted to Obedience

3. **Interactive Prayer:** Addicted to Intimacy

4. **Life Journaling:** Addicted to Change

—— Part Three ——
STEPS TO ADDICTION

Chapter 6:
Focused Thinking: Addicted to Truth

Joshua 1:8
This book of the law shall not depart from your mouth, but you shall meditate on it day and night, so that you may be careful to do according to all that is written in it; for then you will make your way prosperous and then you will have success.

Focused thinking is more than reading the passage; it is meditating on the passage by asking the journalistic questions of who, what, where, when, why and how. I don't have to ask *every* question; I just have to ask the *right* questions. A quality priority time can't be done quickly because it takes time to be a quality journalist. Don't rush your priority time – it is impossible to meditate quickly.

1. Focused thinking asks journalistic questions.

The following are examples of questions you might consider as you go through your priority time:

➤ *Who* wrote it? *Who* said it? *Who* are the major characters? *Who* are the people in the text? To *whom* is the author speaking? About *whom* is he speaking?

➤ *What* is happening in this text? *What* are the main events? In *what* order do they occur? *What* are the major ideas? *What* is the primary point? *What* is the argument? *What* is wrong with this picture? *What* are the blessings of obedience? *What* are the consequences of disobedience?

➤ *Where* is the narrative taking place? *Where* are the people in the story? *Where* are they coming from? *Where* are they going? *Where* is the writer? *Where* were the original readers of this text? *Where* was this done? *Where* was this said? *Where* will it happen?

➤ *When* was it written? *When* did this event take place? *When* did it occur in relation to other events in scripture? *When* did the person say it? *When* did the person do it? *When* will it happen?

➤ *Why* is this included? *Why* is it placed here? *Why* does it follow that? *Why* does it precede that? *Why* was so much or so little space devoted to this particular event or teaching? *Why* was this reference mentioned? *Why* does this person say that? *Why* does that person remain silent? *Why* should they obey? *Why* did they disobey?

➤ *How* did it happen? *How* did the person do that? *How* is this truth illustrated? *How* does this apply to my life?

Remember: Meditation isn't quick, but it's worth it!

2. Focused thinking sees the big picture.

The big picture emphasizes context.
You must understand the context of a verse to interpret it correctly. Correct and confident interpretation must consider the literary, historical, cultural, geographic and theological context. Don't be intimidated by all those words. You can gather most of that information from reading the introduction of each book from a quality study bible, such as the *International Inductive Study Bible*, the *ESV Study Bible* or the *Life Application Study Bible*. In addition, you can also gain some understanding of the context by reading what goes before and what follows after.

The big picture interprets scripture with scripture.
What do you do when you've looked at the context and you're still struggling to understand the scripture? When in doubt, check the cross-references (related verses) and let scripture interpret scripture. There are times when scripture appears to contradict itself, but it never does. If there is an apparent contradiction, there may be more work needed in the observation phase. Detailed and thorough observation leads to correct interpretation. There will also be times you won't understand in the moment. These situations are an opportunity to trust God through the uncertainty until you receive more clarity.

The big picture understands that a verse has one interpretation but many applications.

There is only one correct interpretation of a passage of scripture. The text doesn't mean one thing today and something different tomorrow. Truth is timeless. The first step to accurate application is accurate interpretation. Ephesians 5:25 says, *"Husbands, love your wives, just as Christ Jesus loved the church and gave Himself up for her."* The interpretation is singular, but there are unlimited ways I can apply the truth of loving my wife as Christ loved the church.

3. Focused thinking takes time.

Focused thinking requires *active* reading.

Active reading rarely takes place in your recliner. I recommend having your priority time in a place that promotes good study habits. Focused thinking is never passive; it always requires desire, discipline and determination. I've heard Howard Hendricks say many times, "The bible doesn't yield its fruit to the lazy."

Focused thinking requires *patient* reading.

The goal isn't to read the bible in a year; the goal is to read the bible every day of every year. Reading programs are good for thematic reading, but they emphasize quantity over quality and are not the best option for your priority time. I recommend you start with a book of the bible and patiently work through it.

The type of literature influences the pace of your reading. The Old Testament requires reading longer portions of scripture at a time because it is more historical, biographical or prophetic in nature. In the New Testament, however, I rarely read more than a paragraph or two a day due to the focused style of teaching. I also recommend reading a Psalm or Proverb every evening in addition to your morning priority time because it is another way to meditate on the Word of God day and night.

Focused thinking requires *repetitive* reading.

The discipline of asking journalistic questions requires you to read the passage of scripture multiple times. It is impossible to truly meditate on scripture from a singular reading of the passage. Every observation requires a re-reading of the text; every application takes you back to the text; every prayer should be birthed from the text. Repetitive reading leads to memorization, and this enables you to meditate upon scripture throughout the day.

In the *world*, it only takes one step to develop an addiction, but it takes twelve steps to break one. In the *Word*, it takes longer to develop an addiction, but it is one that cannot easily be broken once you've experienced the transformation that comes from the renewing of your mind. You will never regret being addicted to the Truth.

Chapter 7:
Personal Application: Addicted to Obedience

Matthew 7:24-29

^{24}"Therefore everyone who hears these words of Mine and acts on them, may be compared to a wise man who built his house on the rock. ^{25}And the rain fell, and the floods came, and the winds blew and slammed against that house; and yet it did not fall, for it had been founded on the rock. ^{26}Everyone who hears these words of Mine and does not act on them, will be like a foolish man who built his house on the sand. ^{27}The rain fell, and the floods came, and the winds blew and slammed against that house; and it fell – and great was its fall." ^{28}When Jesus had finished these words, the crowds were amazed at His teaching; ^{29}for He was teaching them as one having authority and not as their scribes.*

Spiritual maturity isn't about discovering the hidden truths; it's about obeying the obvious truths. Before I learned how to have a priority time, I thought the bible was difficult to understand. It isn't difficult to understand; it is difficult to obey.

Application is where your love expresses itself in obedience. It is the decision to quit making excuses and to *"run [the race] in such a way that you may win"* (1 Corinthians 9:24). It is laying aside every weight that slows you down and every sin that causes you to stumble. It is choosing to run the race with endurance. It is focusing your eyes on Jesus, the author and perfecter of your faith. Application is resisting the temptation to grow weary and lose heart. It is the decision to listen and obey. It is the decision to become a man or woman of God.

The importance of application is best communicated by the following equation:

Information + Application = Transformation

1. Personal application is practical.

James 1:22
But prove yourselves doers of the word, and not merely hearers who delude themselves.

Focused thinking is the *hearing* of God's Word; personal application is the *doing* of God's Word. It is impossible to truly know and understand scripture apart from application. "The more you understand it, the more you use it; the more you use it, the more you want to understand it."[2]

Application asks the same journalistic questions that we saw previously in *Focused Thinking* and applies them to your life.

➤ *Why* do I need to apply this truth?
➤ *Where* do I need to apply this truth?
➤ *When* do I need to apply this truth?
➤ *What* other truths do I need to apply?
➤ *How* do I apply this truth?
➤ *Whom* do I need to share this truth with?

Application is personal and practical when it is specific, measurable, attainable, realistic and transferable.

2. Personal application is a responsibility and a reward.

James 4:17
Therefore, to one who knows the right thing to do and does not do it, to him it is sin.

We sin (miss the mark or target) when we disobey the truths we discover. Once we know what a passage means, we are responsible and accountable to obey the truth. Application is simply the principle of sowing and reaping at work. If we sow seeds of obedience, we reap blessings. If we sow seeds of disobedience, we reap consequences. God wants us to be faithful with little so He can put us in charge of more.

We need to apply the principles from the book *QBQ! The Question Behind the Question* to our application. One of the guiding principles of *QBQ* reads, "The answers are in the questions."[3] If we ask a better question, we get a better answer.

Below are some guidelines to help us ask better questions:

> ➤ Start with what or how (NOT why, when or who).
> ➤ Make it personal (NOT they, them, we or you).
> ➤ Focus on action.

Examples:
Ask: What can I do to grow spiritually?
Not: Why isn't attending church enough?

Ask: What can I do to develop myself?
Not: When are they going to train me?

Ask: How can I develop a healthy lifestyle?
Not: Why does cheesecake taste so good?!!

> "We attend too many classes. We buy too many books. We listen to too many podcasts. It's all wasted if we're unclear on what learning really is: Learning is not attending, listening or reading. Nor is it merely gaining knowledge. Learning is really about translating *knowing what to do* into *doing what we know*. It's about changing. If we have not *changed*, we have not *learned*."[3]

What is the responsibility of personal application?

2 Timothy 3:16-17
[16]*All scripture is inspired by God and profitable for teaching, for reproof, for correction, for training in righteousness;* [17]*so that the man of God may be adequate, equipped for every good work.*

These verses give us a responsible framework for personal application.

> ➤ Teaching – What should I *know*?
> ➤ Reproof – What should I *stop*?
> ➤ Correction – What should I *change*?
> ➤ Training – What should I *start*?

What is the reward of personal application?

It is the joy of being used by God to accomplish every good work. Ultimately, the difference between a reward and a regret is personal application. God doesn't reward us for being hearers of the Word but for being doers of the Word (James 1:22).

The Sermon on the Mount (Matthew 5-7) is the sermon of *application*. It isn't about what to know; it's about what to do. Ultimately, it is about wisdom. The wise man hears and acts while the foolish man hears and doesn't act.

Your greatest regrets come from *knowing the truth* yet not *applying the truth*. Look at the following passages and ask yourself, "Do I have an *understanding* problem or an *application* problem?"

Matthew 7:12 – The Golden Rule

"In everything, therefore, treat people the same way you want them to treat you, for this is the Law and the Prophets."

Matthew 22:36-40 – The Great Commandment

[36]"Teacher, which is the great commandment in the Law?" [37]And He said to him, "'You shall love the Lord your God with all your heart and with all your soul and with all your mind.' [38]This is the great and foremost commandment. [39]The second is like it, 'You shall love your neighbor as yourself.' [40]On these two commandments depend the whole Law and the Prophets."

John 13:34-35 – The New Commandment

[34]"A new commandment I give to you, that you love one another, even as I have loved you, that you also love one another. [35]By this all men will know that you are My disciples, if you have love for one another."

Matthew 28:19-20 – The Great Commission

[19]"Go therefore and make disciples of all the nations, baptizing them in the name of the Father and the Son and the Holy Spirit, [20]teaching them to observe all that I commanded you; and lo, I am with you always, even to the end of the age."

Depth according to God isn't about understanding the complexities of the unknown; it's about obeying the simplicity of the known. All of God's truth can be summarized by this equation:

Love God + Love People = Love Works

Chapter 8:
Interactive Prayer: Addicted to Intimacy

Matthew 6:5-8

⁵*"When you pray, you are not to be like the hypocrites; for they love to stand and pray in the synagogues and on the street corners so that they may be seen by men. Truly I say to you, they have their reward in full.* ⁶*But you, when you pray, go into your inner room, close your door and pray to your Father who is in secret, and your Father who sees what is done in secret will reward you.*

⁷*"And when you are praying, do not use meaningless repetition as the Gentiles do, for they suppose that they will be heard for their many words.* ⁸*So do not be like them; for your Father knows what you need before you ask Him."*

Prayer isn't about *talking* as much as it is about *listening*. Because prayer is an expression of relationship, it must be a two-way conversation instead of a monologue. You improve your prayer life by improving your *relationship* and not just your *technique*. Prayer is simple and straightforward; you enjoy listening to and responding to the people you love and respect.

A priority time apart from prayer isn't a priority time; it's simply a bible study. Prayer takes me from an academic experience to a worship experience. It is the key to *relational intimacy* and *life change*. The revelation of God's truth demands a response of confession, repentance and obedience.

1. Interactive prayer is personal.

Matthew 6:5

"When you pray, you are not to be like the hypocrites; for they love to stand and pray in the synagogues and on the street corners so that they may be seen by men. Truly I say to you, they have their reward in full."

What are common characteristics of hypocrites?
They try to *impress* others.
They are *strong in public* but *weak in private*.
They are praying to be *seen by man* instead of *heard by God*.

What are common mistakes in prayer?

➤ **Don't pray in *clichés*.**
  ▷ "Lord, lead, guide and direct us." (Aren't these all saying the same thing?)
  ▷ "Lord, bless the gift and the giver."
  ▷ "Lord, bless this food to the nourishment of my body and my body to Your service." (... especially when I'm eating dessert!)

➤ **Don't pray in *generalities*.**
  ▷ "Lord, forgive me of my sins."
  ▷ "Lord, bless me this day."
  ▷ "Lord, be with Mark and Annika today."

➤ **Don't pray *silently*.**
  ▷ Pray out loud.
  ▷ Pray in posture. (Scripture encourages using different postures such as kneeling.)
  ▷ Write out your prayers. (I know writing is silent, but it is a different kind of silence.)

➤ **Don't pray *selfishly*.**
  ▷ Pray for God's mission.
  ▷ Pray for others' needs.
  ▷ Pray for your needs.

2. Interactive prayer is private.

Matthew 6:6
"But you, when you pray, go into your inner room, close your door and pray to your Father who is in secret, and your Father who sees what is done in secret will reward you."

Private prayer is typically more honest and vulnerable than public prayer. Here are six common characteristics of private prayer:

- You *thank* God more than you *blame* God.
- You *confess* more than you *request*.
- You *listen* more than you *talk*.
- You *react* more than you *act*.
- You *believe* more than you *doubt*.
- You *obey* more than you *disobey*.

3. Interactive prayer is precise.

Matthew 6:7-8
[7]"And when you are praying, do not use meaningless repetition as the Gentiles do, for they suppose that they will be heard for their many words. [8]So do not be like them; for your Father knows what you need before you ask Him."

Pray scripture.
Few things increase my confidence in prayer as much as praying scripture. I'm talking about learning the prayers of the bible and praying specific truths into the context of my life and the lives of my family and friends. Praying scripture is one of the ways we apply scripture. Essentially, what you are doing is observing someone's life and deciding what scripture to pray. It is the primary way that you can be confident that you are praying the will of God into people's lives. What would happen in and through your prayer life if you consistently prayed the prayers of scripture?

Learn the following and begin to pray them for yourself and others:

- The Lord's prayer (Matthew 6:9-15) (Don't just recite it!)
- Christ's intercessory prayer (John 17)
- Paul's prayer for spiritual growth (Ephesians 3:14-22)
- Paul's prayer for knowing God's will (Colossians 1:9-12)
- Paul's prayer for spiritual wisdom (Ephesians 1:15-23)
- Paul's prayer for partners in ministry (Philippians 1:3-11)
- A prayer of praise (Jude 1:24-25)

Here is an example of praying specifically:

Romans 10:1
Brethren, my heart's desire and my prayer to God for them is for their salvation.

Here are some verses that talk about praying with right motives:

James 4:3
You ask and do not receive, because you ask with wrong motives, so that you may spend it on your pleasures.

James 5:16
Therefore, confess your sins to one another and pray for one another so that you may be healed. The effective prayer of a righteous man can accomplish much.

Prayer changes me and others; it invites the presence of God into our priority time. It is through prayer that we are strengthened with His Spirit, grounded in love, able to comprehend the love of Christ and filled up with all the fullness of God (Ephesians 3:14-19).

Chapter 9:
Life Journaling: Addicted to Change

Psalm 23:1-6

¹The LORD is my shepherd, I shall not want. ²He makes me lie down in green pastures; He leads me beside quiet waters. ³He restores my soul; He guides me in the paths of righteousness for His name's sake. ⁴Even though I walk through the valley of the shadow of death, I fear no evil, for You are with me; Your rod and Your staff, they comfort me. ⁵You prepare a table before me in the presence of my enemies; you have anointed my head with oil; my cup overflows. ⁶Surely goodness and loving kindness will follow me all the days of my life, and I will dwell in the house of the LORD forever.

Aren't you glad King David kept a journal? The Psalms are perfect examples of the importance of keeping a journal. They are examples of an honest, transparent and real walk with God. They aren't the journals of a religious man who is trying to impress his readers. They are the journals of a man after God's own heart. We get to experience how David interacted with God through every circumstance of life. We learn from his faith and fears, from his obedience and disobedience, and from his victories and defeats.

Keeping a journal is more than having a diary. I initially thought journaling was for girls! I consistently resisted Clyde's advice to keep a journal and didn't commit to it until after he passed away in the summer of 2000. It isn't something I do at the end of my priority time; it is how I have my priority time.

- ➤ It helps me slow down enough to truly meditate (focused thinking).
- ➤ It helps me in the application phase by forcing me to answer the questions I want to leave unanswered.
- ➤ It helps me to pray specifically, remember my prayers and celebrate the answers.
- ➤ It's where I record my thoughts, evaluate my experiences and capture my memories.

Congratulations! You've just finished the easy part of the book! Now the decision is yours: Are you ready to become addicted to God's Word? I dare you to turn the page...

— Part Four —

START YOUR
ADDICTION

Philippians 1:1-11

¹Paul and Timothy, servants of Christ Jesus,
To all the saints in Christ Jesus who are at Philippi, with the overseers and deacons:
²Grace to you and peace from God our Father and the Lord Jesus Christ.
³I thank my God in all my remembrance of you, ⁴always in every prayer of mine for you all making my prayer with joy, ⁵because of your partnership in the gospel from the first day until now. ⁶And I am sure of this, that he who began a good work in you will bring it to completion at the day of Jesus Christ. ⁷It is right for me to feel this way about you all, because I hold you in my heart, for you are all partakers with me of grace, both in my imprisonment and in the defense and confirmation of the gospel. ⁸For God is my witness, how I yearn for you all with the affection of Christ Jesus. ⁹And it is my prayer that your love may abound more and more, with knowledge and all discernment, ¹⁰so that you may approve what is excellent, and so be pure and blameless for the day of Christ, ¹¹filled with the fruit of righteousness that comes through Jesus Christ, to the glory and praise of God.

FOCUSED THINKING

Notice the journalistic questions (5 W's and 1 H).

1. **What** is Paul thanking God for when he prays for the Philippians?
➤ See 1:5.

2. **What** does Paul pray for the Philippians?
➤ See 1:9-11.

PERSONAL APPLICATION

Application demands specific answers to specific questions. Here are two questions to help you apply the truths from *Focused Thinking*:

1. **How** are you using your strengths and skills to partner in the gospel? Be specific.

2. **What** is one thing you should stop doing and one thing you should start doing in order for your love to abound more and more? Be specific.

INTERACTIVE PRAYER
Write a one paragraph prayer for each application.

LIFE JOURNALING
This whole process is journaling. However, this is also a place to record additional thoughts and capture your memories.

Devotional:
Partnership in the Gospel

What causes you to remember people? What makes you grateful for people? What is so positive and promising that you would remember people in prayer with joy? Let's be brutally honest for a moment. Most of our prayers are about ourselves and our families. Something significant has to happen in order for someone else to consistently be included in our prayer life.

There are many reasons why this is true. Most people spend less than five minutes per day in prayer; therefore, you have to be incredibly special to make someone's five-minute list! Besides adversity and crisis, what pushes people to the top of your prayer list? It is *partnership*. They have partnered with you in a positive way. They have come alongside you and helped you. They have helped you be a better version of yourself or helped you accomplish one of your goals. In other words, they have made a difference in your life or in the lives of people you love.

What caused Paul to pray so passionately for the Philippians? It was because of their *partnership* in the gospel from the first day until now (1:5). This partnership was deeply personal because they *partnered* with Paul through his *"imprisonment and confirmation of the gospel"* (1:7). They believed in Paul when others doubted him. They were loyal when others compromised. There isn't a deeper bond than the bond of persevering through trials and pressing on toward a shared goal.

This is why Paul says, *"It is right for me to **feel** this way about you all."* He says, *"I hold you in my **heart**, for you are all **partakers** with me of grace"* (1:7). How would you feel about friends who stood with you through adversity? How would you feel about friends who stayed true to the mission regardless of the opposition? This is why Paul could say, *"I am sure of this, that he who began a good work in you will bring it to completion at the day of Jesus Christ"* (1:6). Paul was confident because they had already persevered; they had already proven themselves. They had already been faithful with a little; they could be trusted with more. They had already fought the good fight; they could be trusted to keep fighting.

Paul was proud of them because they were his disciples. They were his learners and followers. They were following him just as he was following Christ. They were imitating him just as he was imitating Christ. Paul was like a proud parent, a proud coach or a proud leader. His greatest successes were not his accomplishments; his greatest successes were the accomplishments of his followers. This is why Paul could say, *"For God is my witness, how I yearn for you all with all the **affection** of Christ Jesus"* (1:8). Paul loved his *partners* in the gospel more than he loved anyone or anything in life apart from Christ.

PERSONAL APPLICATION

1. Are you partnering in the mission?
2. Who are your partners in the mission?

Look at Paul's prayer for his *"partners in the gospel"*:

"And it is my prayer that your love may abound more and more, with knowledge and all discernment, so that you may approve what is excellent, and so be pure and blameless for the day of Christ, filled with the fruit of righteousness that comes through Jesus Christ, to the glory and praise of God" (1:9-11).

How would you like to have that prayer consistently prayed for you? What would happen if you consistently prayed that prayer for others? That prayer represents the heart of a parent, a pastor and a partner. Try to write a more complete prayer than that prayer. What do you need more of for your love to abound more and more with knowledge and all discernment? Why do you need that prayer to be answered? *"[S]o that you may approve what is excellent, and so be pure and blameless for the day of Christ, filled with the fruit of righteousness"* (1:10-11). Seriously, how good does that sound?

Philippians 1:12-14

[12]I want you to know, brothers, that what has happened to me has really served to advance the gospel, [13]so that it has become known throughout the whole imperial guard and to all the rest that my imprisonment is for Christ. [14]And most of the brothers, having become confident in the Lord by my imprisonment, are much more bold to speak the word without fear.

FOCUSED THINKING

Notice the journalistic questions (5 W's and 1 H).

1. **How** did Paul's imprisonment (1:7) serve to advance the gospel?
   ➤ See 1:13.

2. **What** has been the result of Paul's imprisonment on most of the brothers?
   ➤ See 1:14.

PERSONAL APPLICATION

Application demands specific answers to specific questions. Here are two questions to help you apply the truths from *Focused Thinking*:

1. **How** has God used your adversity through the years to advance the gospel? Be specific.

2. **How** has your perseverance through adversity created boldness in others? Be specific.

INTERACTIVE PRAYER

Write a one paragraph prayer for each application.

LIFE JOURNALING

This whole process is journaling. However, this is also a place to record additional thoughts and capture your memories.

Devotional:
Advance the Gospel

Have you ever noticed that almost every great movie starts with a problem, with some type of adversity? Why is that? Nothing captures your attention like a problem. The storyteller sets the dilemma for the purpose of you identifying with the problem on an emotional level. He or she is creating an emotional attachment with the character so that you want to help solve the problem.

In this particular story, Paul has gone from *persecutor* of the church, to *preacher* for the church, to *imprisonment* for his commitment to the church. However, Paul is using his adversity to advance the gospel. Be honest: How would you feel if you were imprisoned for doing good? How unfair, right? There are few things we complain about more than "bad things happening to good people." I understand why we think this way, but this thinking neglects to understand that we are sinful people living in a sinful, fallen world. Bad things are the norm in this world, not the exception. God doesn't promise us a problem-free life in this sinful world, but He does strengthen us to persevere and press on.

What was Paul's attitude about his imprisonment? He trusted God with his circumstances, even adverse circumstances. Not only did he trust God, but he also chose to make the best of his situation. He didn't see the imperial guards as his prison guards; he saw them as future followers of Christ. They became a captive audience to witness his life, read his letters and hear his stories about Christ. Paul was committed to turn his obstacles into opportunities.

PERSONAL APPLICATION
1. What role does adversity play in *your* life?
2. Do you see yourself as the victim?

Unfortunately, the victim mentality is far too common today. In a fallen world, there are times in life when we legitimately are the victim. However, the majority of the time, we simply reap what we sow. It's time for us to flip the switch and see our circumstances from God's perspective. Instead of complaining about them, try to find Christ in and through your circumstances.

God is the only One you can trust to ultimately cause all things to work together for good. Complaining about the circumstance doesn't change the circumstance. Finding God's perspective and choosing to persevere not only has the potential to change the circumstance, but it also changes you and others through it. It wasn't Paul's imprisonment that changed the imperial guards and his brothers in the faith; it was Paul's response to his imprisonment that changed them. *"And most of the brothers, having become **confident** in the Lord **by my imprisonment**, are **much more bold to speak** the word **without fear**"* (1:14).

Our response to circumstances and crisis is frequently our most persuasive and powerful testimony to others. Anybody can love the Lord in a season of blessing, but what about in a season of adversity? There is something about the process of perseverance that purifies us. When we are weak, He is strong. It is important to remember that most people find Christ in the crisis.

Unfortunately, we don't live life on the mountain top. The good news is that we don't live it in the valley, either. We live the majority of life going up and down the mountain. It is important for people to see Christ in you through every phase of the journey.

Priority Time:
Day 3 of 21

Philippians 1:15-18

15Some indeed preach Christ from envy and rivalry, but others from good will. 16The latter do it out of love, knowing that I am put here for the defense of the gospel. 17The former proclaim Christ out of selfish ambition, not sincerely but thinking to afflict me in my imprisonment. 18What then? Only that in every way, whether in pretense or in truth, Christ is proclaimed, and in that I rejoice.
Yes, and I will rejoice...

FOCUSED THINKING

Notice the journalistic questions (5 W's and 1 H).

1. **What** are the motives driving people to preach Christ?
➤ See 1:15.

2. **How** does Paul respond to pure, and less than pure, motives?
➤ See 1:18.

PERSONAL APPLICATION

Application demands specific answers to specific questions. Here are two questions to help you apply the truths from *Focused Thinking*:

1. **How** do you respond to people preaching Christ with less than pure motives? Be specific.

2. **What** perspective do you need in order to rejoice regardless of motive? Be specific.

INTERACTIVE PRAYER

Write a one paragraph prayer for each application.

LIFE JOURNALING

This whole process is journaling. However, this is also a place to record additional thoughts and capture your memories.

Devotional:
Rejoice Regardless

Almost every profession in life has those who are in it for the right reasons and those who are in it for the wrong reasons. Few things in life gain my disrespect more than people who make their careers and success all about themselves. That is true in business, sports and entertainment, but it is especially true in ministry. How do you feel toward people who *"preach Christ from envy and rivalry"*? How do you feel toward people who are not "sincere" in their proclamation of Christ?

These questions feel like they should generate a negative feeling and response. Are there specific people who pop into your mind when you read those questions? How do you feel about those people? Are you disappointed in them? Do you respect them? When I flip through the channels and run across TV preachers, I have to admit that my first thought is negative and critical. In fact, if I'm really honest, I feel that spirit of the self-righteous Pharisee rise up inside of me. I literally have to change the channel or I'll slip into the comparison game and make it all about me.

Take notice of the questions we ask and how we indirectly make the whole situation about us.

1. "Why is someone like that on TV?"
   ➤ What am I really saying? "Why is *that* person on TV instead of me?"
2. "Why don't people see that he or she is fake?"
   ➤ What am I really saying? "Why don't people see that I'm real?"
3. "How can *that* person be *that* successful?"
   ➤ What am I really saying? "How can that person be more successful than me?"

Are you ever amazed by your own sinfulness? Time and time again, sin expresses itself through my life when I feel the desire to judge or be critical of others. When I put others down, I'm actually attempting to lift myself up. In that moment I become guilty of the *"envy and rivalry"* that offended me in the first place. Oftentimes, what I dislike in others is really what I dislike about myself.

What was Paul's perspective on people who preached Christ *"from envy and rivalry"*? He didn't focus on the person preaching; he focused on the opportunity for people to hear the message of Christ. He didn't make it about the *preacher*; he made it about the *message*. As long as the message was Christ, he rejoiced. Why? The hope of the world is Christ, not perfect preachers. In fact, none of us are holy enough, loving enough or real enough to earn the right to preach Christ. However, by God's grace we should strive to be above reproach and do everything possible to model the life of Christ.

Let's make an agreement together: Let's not judge the motives of people's hearts. Typically, the moment we judge someone's motive is the moment we become guilty of the very sins we are judging. There is an appropriate place for developmental feedback. There is a time, place and way to evaluate truth and fight against heresy. But if Christ is being preached, don't judge the motives; simply rejoice. Why? Because it's not about the preacher; it's about the receiver.

PERSONAL APPLICATION

1. Where are you judging someone's motives?
2. How do you put people down in order to lift yourself up?
3. What do you need to do to make those relationships right?

Philippians 1:19-20

[19][F]or I know that through your prayers and the help of the Spirit of Jesus Christ this will turn out for my deliverance, [20]as it is my eager expectation and hope that I will not be at all ashamed, but that with full courage now as always Christ will be honored in my body, whether by life or by death.

FOCUSED THINKING

Notice the journalistic questions (5 W's and 1 H).

1. **What** is Paul depending on for his deliverance?
➤ See 1:19.

2. **What** is Paul's hope, regardless of his circumstances?
➤ See 1:20.

PERSONAL APPLICATION

Application demands specific answers to specific questions. Here are two questions to help you apply the truths from *Focused Thinking*:

1. **Who** needs you to pray for them to be delivered from a difficult circumstance? Be specific.

2. **What** is the most determined you've ever been to honor Christ, regardless of your circumstances? Be specific.

INTERACTIVE PRAYER

Write a one paragraph prayer for each application.

LIFE JOURNALING

This whole process is journaling. However, this is also a place to record additional thoughts and capture your memories.

Devotional:
Responding to Adversity

What do you typically do when you find yourself in a crisis? Whether you are a person of prayer or not, you pray. I wish this wasn't true, but nothing causes me to pray more than when there's pain. God prefers to change us by purpose and pleasure, but He loves us enough to also change us through pain.

How do *you* respond to adversity? Have you ever asked the question, "Why me?" Most of the time, hardship simply reveals the presence or absence of character. However, from God's perspective, adversity is an opportunity to *develop* your character. More often than not, defining moments are determined by our response to difficulties. Think about it this way: You are who you are today because of your responses to adversity. Paul wasn't Paul because of the *absence* of hardship in his life; Paul became Paul because of his *response* to hardship in his life. Paul allowed God to use circumstances and crises to develop his character.

Most people misunderstand God because they misunderstand circumstances. They think a good God must provide good circumstances. They don't understand that "The Fall" has made it impossible for God to provide good circumstances *and* free will at the same time. We must quit blaming God for circumstances and start seeing God in and through them. Here's the reality: Most adverse circumstances are created by *us*, not God. We aren't promised a problem-free life, but He does promise to cause all things to work together for good.

We could not become who we are becoming today without the problems of yesterday. Instead of questioning God or blaming people for his problems, Paul chose to persevere and press on. It's important to understand that problems are normal, but God's perspective regarding our problems is abnormal. How did Paul's adversity of prison turn out for the advancement of the gospel? Everything about Paul's attitude and actions was a witness to the Praetorian Guard and strengthened the believers to speak the Word of God without fear.

How are *you* going to respond to adversity? You can't avoid it in life; therefore, choose to persevere and press on. If you can't obey God in adversity, you won't obey God in prosperity.

PERSONAL APPLICATION

What are three examples of adversity that have developed your character?

Philippians 1:21-26

21For to me to live is Christ, and to die is gain. 22If I am to live in the flesh, that means fruitful labor for me. Yet which I shall choose I cannot tell. 23I am hard pressed between the two. My desire is to depart and be with Christ, for that is far better. 24But to remain in the flesh is more necessary on your account. 25Convinced of this, I know that I will remain and continue with you all, for your progress and joy in the faith, 26so that in me you may have ample cause to glory in Christ Jesus, because of my coming to you again.

FOCUSED THINKING
Notice the journalistic questions (5 W's and 1 H).

1. **What** is Paul's definition of life?
➤ See 1:21.

2. **What** happens when Christ is your life?
➤ See 1:22-25.

PERSONAL APPLICATION
Application demands specific answers to specific questions. Here are two questions to help you apply the truths from *Focused Thinking*:

1. **What** is the definition of your life? Be specific.

2. **How** do you live for the "*progress and joy in the faith*" of others? If you don't, what is one simple way you can start? Be specific.

INTERACTIVE PRAYER
Write a one paragraph prayer for each application.

LIFE JOURNALING
This whole process is journaling. However, this is also a place to record additional thoughts and capture your memories.

Devotional:
For me to live is _____

- ➤ Who is closest to you in life?
- ➤ What would he or she say you are the most passionate about?
- ➤ What gives you the most energy?
- ➤ What finds its way onto your calendar regardless of how busy you are?

You know the answers to these questions, but you are biased in your answers. You have the "Positive Illusion Factor" working, where you see the issues more positively because you are passionate about them. However, you need to hear the non-biased answers from your family and friends.

How did this happen in Paul's life? He had many people who respected and loved him. He was close to people because of his investment in them and their churches. However, this passage of scripture represents two years in the Philippian jail. He didn't have access to his friends like before, but he was close to the Praetorian Guard. It wasn't the same type of closeness at first: he was chained to members of the guard day and night; he couldn't go to the restroom in privacy, couldn't sleep in privacy, and couldn't even pray in privacy. He was in a very demoralizing and dehumanizing situation, yet he did not get discouraged or dissuaded.

Who knew Paul the best during his two years in jail? The guards were with him non-stop; therefore, they became qualified to answer the questions we asked in the first paragraph. They had a unique perspective because they got to witness how Paul responded to adversity. They had a front row seat to evaluating what Paul's life was *really* about.

How did Paul define his quality of life? Life for Paul wasn't about position, possessions or pleasures. If you have a proper definition of life, you can face and overcome any circumstance. Paul knew that life isn't about *circumstances*; life is about *Christ*. This is why Philippians 1:21-22 says, *"For to me to live is Christ, and to die is gain. If I am to live in the flesh, that means fruitful labor for me. Yet which I shall choose I cannot tell."* Let me make that extremely clear and break it down into two statements:

1. For me to live is Christ.
2. For me to live is fruitful labor.

What is fruitful labor? It doesn't have to be a different type of labor from your norm; often, it is the same labor but with Christ's purpose in and through it. For example, if Jesus did your job, how would He do it? He wouldn't become the "cheesy Christian" in the workplace, but He *would* model character, excellence and friendship. He would make time to pray for people, serve people and ultimately prove that love works.

What are examples of fruitful labor in your life? How do you spend your time? How do you spend your money? Are you applying God's purpose to your work? Are you applying God's love to your marriage and parenting? Are you serving according to your strengths to accomplish God's mission?

Paul has a win-win situation in front of him, but notice what he chooses: "*I am hard pressed between the two. My desire is to depart and be with Christ, for that is far better. But to remain in the flesh is more necessary on your account. Convinced of this, I know that I will remain and continue with you all, for your progress and joy in the faith*" (1:23-25).

1. Who needs you to live for them?
2. Who are you living for?
3. Who would say you are committed to their progress and joy in the faith?

Life isn't about me; it is about loving God and people. Others need your faithfulness and fruitful labor; others need your perseverance and pressing on. It is vitally important for us to realize that Christianity isn't a way of *thinking*; it is a way of *living*. Others need us to live for their progress and joy in the faith.

What are the results of living for Christ and others? Philippians 1:26 says, "[S]o that in me you may have ample cause to glory in *Christ Jesus, because of my coming to you again.*" Do you give glory to Christ because of the ways that you live for the progress and joy of others in the faith? That's the ultimate source of satisfaction and fulfillment in this life.

PERSONAL APPLICATION

1. Who are the three closest people to you?
2. What would they say you are the most passionate about?
3. Fill in the blank (not the biblical answer, but the current reality): *"For me to live is* _____*."*

Philippians 1:27-30

[27]Only let your manner of life be worthy of the gospel of Christ, so that whether I come and see you or am absent, I may hear of you that you are standing firm in one spirit, with one mind striving side by side for the faith of the gospel, [28]and not frightened in anything by your opponents. This is a clear sign to them of their destruction, but of your salvation, and that from God. [29]For it has been granted to you that for the sake of Christ you should not only believe in him but also suffer for his sake, [30]engaged in the same conflict that you saw I had and now hear that I still have.

FOCUSED THINKING
Notice the journalistic questions (5 W's and 1 H).

1. **What** does it look like for your manner of life to be worthy of the gospel of Christ?
➤ See 1:27-28.

2. **What** does this passage say about suffering?
➤ See 1:30.

PERSONAL APPLICATION
Application demands specific answers to specific questions. Here are two questions to help you apply the truths from *Focused Thinking*:

1. **How** do you walk in a manner worthy of the gospel of Christ? Be specific.

2. **How** have you or others you know suffered for the sake of Christ? Be specific.

INTERACTIVE PRAYER
Write a one paragraph prayer for each application.

LIFE JOURNALING

This whole process is journaling. However, this is also a place to record additional thoughts and capture your memories.

Devotional:
A Life that is Worthy

If your best friend died for you, how would that influence your choices in life? Would you be driven to live in a manner that was worthy of his or her life? It would be impossible not to feel a sense of responsibility. Though salvation is free to us, it is costly to God. Jesus died for us so that we could live for Him. He died so that we could live a life that is worthy of the gospel of Christ.

Do you feel the weight of that statement? Paul doesn't want you to feel it in a burdensome way, he wants you to feel it in an inspirational way. It isn't about pressure; it's about the privilege of life and life more abundant. He is exhorting us and encouraging us to live a life that glorifies God by standing firm in one spirit. In other words, don't be led astray by other people, by other teachings or by adversity. Standing firm isn't an easy task, but it is definitely better than not standing firm. Here's the way I like to think about it: In this sinful, fallen world life is going to be a fight whether you live for God or not; therefore, why not choose to fight the good fight?

Speaking of fighting, notice what Paul says next: "*...with one mind striving side by side for the faith of the gospel*" (1:27). Where does the word "striving" fit into your understanding of your walk with God. Unfortunately, most Christians today incorrectly think that Christianity should be easy. However, that view is inconsistent with scripture. We are constantly striving against the sinful desires of our flesh and against the schemes of the devil. This is why Ephesians 6 teaches us about putting on the whole armor of God. It is also important to note that we should strive side by side for the faith of the gospel. It's too difficult to strive alone. We must strive as soldiers in God's army to win God's battle. The battle is too great for any one of us to handle alone.

I love how Paul says that the Philippians are "*not frightened in anything by [their] opponents*" (1:28). It's amazing how confident we can be when we know that God and God's people are on our side. Nothing threatens the enemy more than God's people standing firm, having one mind and striving side by side for the faith of the gospel. How many churches do you know where that is an accurate description of the people? Unfortunately, I don't know of many today, but I want to be this type of church.

The last two verses of this passage are proof that man didn't write the bible without the leading and authority of the Holy Spirit. Philippians 1:29-30 says, *"For it has been granted to you that for the sake of Christ you should not only believe in him but also suffer for his sake, engaged in the same conflict that you saw I had and now hear that I still have."* Man would never write something like this because man never wants to suffer! However, instead of being *discouraged* by this statement, I'm *encouraged* by its honesty. I'd rather live in the reality of the fight than live in the disappointment of a false reality. No one enjoys suffering, but at least our suffering has purpose and will end in pleasure one day. Therefore, it is our responsibility to persevere and *"press on toward the goal for the prize of the upward call of God in Christ Jesus"* (Philippians 3:14).

PERSONAL APPLICATION

1. What adjustments do you need to make to stand firm in your faith?
2. What adjustments do you need to make to have one mind with God?
3. What adjustments do you need to make to strive side by side for the faith of the gospel?

Philippians 2:1-4

1So if there is any encouragement in Christ, any comfort from love, any participation in the Spirit, any affection and sympathy, 2complete my joy by being of the same mind, having the same love, being in full accord and of one mind. 3Do nothing from selfish ambition or conceit, but in humility count others more significant than yourselves. 4Let each of you look not only to his own interests, but also to the interests of others.

FOCUSED THINKING

Notice the journalistic questions (5 W's and 1 H).

1. **What** completes Paul's joy?
➤ See 2:2.

2. **How** should we treat others?
➤ See 2:3-4.

PERSONAL APPLICATION

Application demands specific answers to specific questions. Here are two questions to help you apply the truths from *Focused Thinking*:

1. **What** are three ways you can strive toward unity? Be specific.

2. **What** are three ways you can prioritize the interests of others? Be specific.

INTERACTIVE PRAYER

Write a one paragraph prayer for each application.

LIFE JOURNALING

This whole process is journaling. However, this is also a place to record additional thoughts and capture your memories.

Devotional:
The Humility Factor

This passage is one of my favorites for many reasons, but one primary reason is that I can hear the voice of my mentor through it. Clyde Cranford used to say that this is one of the easiest passages in the bible to understand, but one of the most difficult to obey. Before we get to the difficulty of verses 3 and 4, let's look at the first two verses.

The word "if" can also be translated "since," so let's read verse 1 this way:

- ➤ *"**Since** there is encouragement in Christ..."*
- ➤ *"**Since** there is comfort from love..."*
- ➤ *"**Since** there is participation in the Spirit..."*
- ➤ *"**Since** there is affection and sympathy..."*

Do you have encouragement, comfort, participation, affection and sympathy in your walk with God? These qualities should inspire you to complete the joy of your pastoral leaders. Are you giving from what you are receiving? God fills us up for the purpose of pouring us out. For example, it's great to receive joy, but it's even greater to give joy.

How does Paul instruct the Philippians to complete his joy? *"Complete my joy by being of the same mind, having the same love, being in full accord and of one mind"* (2:2). Do you see the emphasis on unity? Few things in life bring parents more joy than unity among their children. In the same way, few things bring pastors more joy than unity among their members. Unity isn't the norm with sinful people; true unity is only achieved when people are of the same mind and same love.

Now we arrive at one of the most difficult verses in the bible to obey: *"Do nothing from selfish ambition or conceit, but in humility count others more significant than yourselves. Let each of you look not only to his own interest, but also to the interests of others"* (2:3-4). Let's make this really simple: When you think about dinner, do you think about what *you* want first or about what your spouse or friend wants first? When it comes to my taste buds, I always think of me first! It's amazing how persuasive and powerful our taste buds are when they join forces together.

Let's take it a step further: When you think about entertainment, do you think about what *you* want first or about what your spouse or friend wants first? Again, that's an easy answer.

Let me ask you a question that will reveal the magnitude of our selfishness: What are your most unreasonable expressions of selfishness?

Selfishness means hyper-fighting or spirit of rivalry. It is fighting for *your* desires and preferences over the desires and preferences of others. Most people think the solution to selfishness is generosity; but the real solution is to replace pride with humility. Here's the bottom line: Prideful people are selfish people. This is why it is so important for us to see Jesus describe Himself as humble in Matthew 11:29: "*Take my yoke upon you, and learn from me, for I am gentle* [meek] *and lowly* [humble] *in heart, and you will find rest for your souls.*" Jesus is telling us to learn how to have strength under control and be humble. Humility isn't thinking less of yourself; it is thinking more of God and accurately of yourself.

Paul is warning his healthiest and most generous church against pride and its expressions of selfishness. It's always easier to be divided instead of united, critical instead of complimentary, and greedy instead of generous. When someone is prideful or conceited, they are trying to create their own glory. It is an attempt to create importance, but it is in vain. Our desire to be important tempts us to be selfish and fight for *our* interests instead of the interests of those around us.

What are the results of pride and selfishness? You become boring because you always talk about yourself and you always do what *you* want to do. Check out this principle: The more important you act, the less important you become. How do we reverse this terrible problem? How do God's people create importance? Two primary ways: First, you become important by making others important. Second, you become lovable by loving others.

PERSONAL APPLICATION

1. When you make yourself important, you create separation from God and people.
    ➤ Prideful people are selfish people.
    ➤ Selfish people are lonely people.

2. When you make others important, you create intimacy with God and people.
   - ➤ Humble people are giving people.
   - ➤ Giving people are lovable people.

3. What's the difference between earthly and eternal importance?
   - ➤ Earthly importance is based upon *who serves you.*
   - ➤ Eternal importance is based upon *whom you serve.*

Philippians 2:5-11

[5]*Have this mind among yourselves, which is yours in Christ Jesus,* [6]*who, though he was in the form of God, did not count equality with God a thing to be grasped,* [7]*but emptied himself, by taking the form of a servant, being born in the likeness of men.* [8]*And being found in human form, he humbled himself by becoming obedient to the point of death, even death on a cross.* [9]*Therefore God has highly exalted him and bestowed on him the name that is above every name,* [10]*so that at the name of Jesus every knee should bow, in heaven and on earth and under the earth,* [11]*and every tongue confess that Jesus Christ is Lord, to the glory of God the Father.*

FOCUSED THINKING

Notice the journalistic questions (5 W's and 1 H).

1. **How** does Paul describe the mind/attitude of Christ?
➤ See 2:6-8.

2. **What** position has God given Jesus for humbling Himself?
➤ See 2:9-11.

PERSONAL APPLICATION

Application demands specific answers to specific questions. Here are two questions to help you apply the truths from *Focused Thinking*:

1. **What** do you need to do to increase and improve the mind of Christ in you? Be specific.

2. **What** are two things you can do to humble yourself? Be specific.

INTERACTIVE PRAYER

Write a one paragraph prayer for each application.

LIFE JOURNALING

This whole process is journaling. However, this is also a place to record additional thoughts and capture your memories.

Devotional:
Attitude

What attitude did you bring into work today? What attitude are you bringing home today? Most people have a high attitude awareness of others, but not of themselves. Attitude is essential because it determines how you perceive your world and how your world perceives you.

Your attitude isn't determined by your circumstances; it is determined by your choices. It is convenient to blame our attitude on our circumstances, but we must rise above them. Many factors influence your attitude, but it should be determined by having the mind of Christ in you. The driving influencer in the mind of Christ is the spirit of humility. Humility is the foundation from an attitude perspective. If you operate from a position of humility instead of pride, then your attitude is to consider others as more important than yourself. That's not a statement of inequality; rather, it is a statement of one person prioritizing the needs and preferences of another person over his or her own.

If our attitude was determined by circumstances, then Jesus should have had a bad attitude. His three and a half years of public ministry were full of many highs, but He faced constant challenges and crises. The key is to realize it's not what happens to you that matters, it's how you choose to respond to the things that happen. Health and happiness aren't determined by the absence of problems, but by your response to problems.

How did Jesus respond? "*[T]hough he was in the form of God, [he] did not count equality with God a thing to be grasped, but emptied himself, by taking the form of a servant, being born in the likeness of men. And being found in human form, he humbled himself by becoming obedient to the point of death, even death on a cross*" (2:6-8). How hard is it to "make yourself nothing?" How hard is it to take the form of a servant, especially when you're the King of kings? Jesus trusted the voice of His Father over the confusion of the circumstances. He didn't define who *God* was or who *He* was based upon circumstances. He focused on the victory instead of the defeat. He knew certain battles had to be lost in order to win the war. It is important for us to realize that we can't have the produce without the process. God uses the process to produce the product. Most of our learning doesn't happen in the classroom; it happens through the journey of life.

What could you endure and overcome if you knew victory awaited you on the other side? What would you say to yourself about the circumstances you're facing? What would your attitude be toward the adversity? Jesus *trusted* the promises of His Father before He *experienced* them.

Therefore God has highly exalted him and bestowed on him the name that is above every name, so that at the name of Jesus every knee should bow, in heaven and on earth and under the earth, and every tongue confess that Jesus Christ is Lord, to the glory of God the Father. (2:9-11)

Regardless of how bad it gets in this world, our attitude must be determined by the promises of God. We've already won the war, but we still have to fight. It is the mind of Christ that enables your attitude to be determined by *promises* instead of *problems*.

PERSONAL APPLICATION
1. Where do you struggle the most in your attitude?
2. What do you need to do to replace pride with humility?
3. What do you need to do to focus on promises instead of problems?

Philippians 2:12-13

[12]Therefore, my beloved, as you have always obeyed, so now, not only as in my presence but much more in my absence, work out your own salvation with fear and trembling, [13]for it is God who works in you, both to will and to work for his good pleasure.

FOCUSED THINKING

Notice the journalistic questions (5 W's and 1 H).

1. **Who** is at work in you?
➤ See 2:13.

2. **How** does God work through you to accomplish His good pleasure?
➤ Since this one is not intuitive, be patient; you can find the answer in today's devotional.

PERSONAL APPLICATION

Application demands specific answers to specific questions. Here are two questions to help you apply the truths from *Focused Thinking*:

1. **How** do you work out your salvation with fear and trembling? Be specific.

2. **How** can you use your strengths to please Him the most? Be specific.

INTERACTIVE PRAYER

Write a one paragraph prayer for each application.

LIFE JOURNALING

This process is journaling; however, this is also a place to record your thoughts and capture your memories.

Devotional:
Work Required

Have you ever noticed that a lot of Christians aren't growing? Unfortunately, many followers of Christ appear to do more *attending* than following. I believe most Christians have the best of intentions, but not the best results. What's missing? Work is missing. It's really that simple. Let me explain...

Most Christians misunderstand the role of work in their Christian experience. It is important to distinguish the difference between work before salvation and work after salvation. Salvation is a free gift to us, but it was earned by Jesus' work on the cross. It is *His* work that saves us, not *our* work. Here's the bottom line of salvation: We are saved by grace through faith in Christ alone.

Now that we are absolutely certain and clear that salvation isn't by works, let's reorient ourselves to the word "work." Philippians 2:12b says, *"[W]ork out your salvation with fear and trembling..."* What does that mean? It doesn't sound negative; in fact, it sounds like something we should embrace. Paul is telling us to work *out* what God has already worked *in*. It requires work for us to grow through the seven stages of life physically and spiritually.

1. Babes (1 Corinthians 3:1; Hebrews 5:13)
2. Little Children (Galatians 4:19; 1 John 2:1)
3. Children (2 Corinthians 6:13, 12:14; Ephesians 4:14)
4. Young Men (Titus 2:6; 1 John 2:13)
5. Men or Fathers (1 Corinthians 4:15, 16:13; 2 Timothy 2:2)
6. Elders (1 Timothy 5:17; 1 Peter 5:1)
7. Aged (Titus 2:2; Philemon 9)

The word "work" means "energize" or "provide enablement." Who provides the energy or enablement for you to work? Philippians 2:13 says, *"[F]or it is God who works in you, both to will and to work for his good pleasure."* There is nothing negative about work, especially when you understand that you are working according to God's work in you. All work is orchestrated by the power of the Holy Spirit. It is God's Spirit that creates the desire (will) to work for God's good pleasure. John 15:5 clearly explains that apart from Him we can do nothing.

Work in salvation and sanctification is initiated and fueled by the Holy Spirit, but it still requires effort. Dallas Willard explained it best when he said, "Grace is not opposed to effort; it is opposed to earning."[4] Spiritual growth (or the more theological term, *sanctification*) has always required work and will always require work. In fact, it is a stewardship issue. It is our responsibility to be good stewards of our salvation by "*working out [our] salvation with fear and trembling*" (2:12).

The picture of the farmer illustrates God's role and our role perfectly. First and foremost, we must understand that God created, and operates by, the law of the harvest. You reap what you sow. It is the farmer's responsibility to plow the soil, prepare the seedbed, plant the seed and pray for rain. This is where the farmer's faith intersects with God's faithfulness. The farmer does what only he can do and trusts God to do what only He can do: Bring the rain. Everything with God is relational, but relationships require work. They are fueled, nurtured and sustained by love; but love only works when *you* work.

PERSONAL APPLICATION

1. Where are you working in your love relationship with Christ?
2. What are the results of that work?
3. Where do you need to work more in your love relationship with Christ?

Philippians 2:14-18

[14]Do all things without grumbling or disputing, [15]that you may be blameless and innocent, children of God without blemish in the midst of a crooked and twisted generation, among whom you shine as lights in the world, [16]holding fast to the word of life, so that in the day of Christ I may be proud that I did not run in vain or labor in vain. [17]Even if I am to be poured out as a drink offering upon the sacrificial offering of your faith, I am glad and rejoice with you all. [18]Likewise you also should be glad and rejoice with me.

FOCUSED THINKING

Notice the journalistic questions (5 W's and 1 H).

1. **What** are we to do without grumbling or questioning?
➤ See 2:14.

2. **What** should be the characteristics of godly men and women?
➤ See 2:15-16.

PERSONAL APPLICATION

Application demands specific answers to specific questions. Here are two questions to help you apply the truths from *Focused Thinking*:

1. **What** do you grumble or complain about the most? Be specific.

2. **What** do you need to do to run to win instead of run in vain? Be specific.

INTERACTIVE PRAYER

Write a one paragraph prayer for each application.

LIFE JOURNALING

This whole process is journaling. However, this is also a place to record additional thoughts and capture your memories.

Devotional:
Don't Just Stop It; Start it!

What do you complain about? If you don't know, ask your co-workers or those closest to you. It's my educated guess that all of us complain more than we realize. I hate complainers, yet I complain. Why do I loath it in others, but give myself a pass? I think our culture has adopted an attitude that says it's socially acceptable to complain. In fact, we expect it and find ourselves surprised, even shocked, when people consistently have a positive attitude.

An attitude of positivity is so rare that I prioritize it in our hiring process at Highpoint Church. Listen to this description of a person who has the strength of positivity: "You are generous with praise, quick to smile, and always on the lookout for the positive in the situation. You are a person who sees the glass as half full. As a result of your energy, enthusiasm and encouragement people want to be around you."[5] I want to meet that person, don't you? Who are the people in your circle of life who are known for their positivity? How many of those people are Christians?

Unfortunately, not many Christians are known for their positive attitudes toward people and life. God will never win the world through grumpy people! This is one of the many reasons why He says, *"Do all things without grumbling or disputing"* (2:14). A watching world needs to see us be people who are *"blameless and innocent, children of God without blemish in the midst of a crooked and twisted generation, among whom [we] shine as lights in the world"* (2:15). You aren't shining when you're complaining. *Stop* letting your circumstances determine your attitude; *start* letting Christ determine your attitude. In John 15:11 Jesus says, *"These things I have spoken to you, that my joy may be in you, and that your joy may be full."* It is time for people to experience Christ's joy in us and through us, regardless of our circumstances.

How do I do that? Philippians 1:16 says, *"[H]olding fast to the word of life, so that in the day of Christ I may be proud that I did not run in vain or labor in vain."* The Word of God is the anchor that holds through any storm. It is the foundation of transformation. Without the Word of God, all of us will be unattractive complainers. It is the promises of the Word of God past, present and future that inspire us to persevere and press on. Otherwise, it's too easy to quit running. However, the secret to running instead of quitting is to keep your eyes focused on Jesus as the author and perfecter of your faith.

PERSONAL APPLICATION

What's the best way to quit complaining? Here's the best application I can give you for the next 11 days of this 21 days of priority times: Replace complaining with complimenting. Don't just stop complaining – that's not good enough. The goal isn't to just stop negativity and become neutral. The goal is to replace negativity with positivity. This is one of the many ways you can be poured out as a drink offering and cause others to be glad and rejoice with you.

Philippians 2:19-24

[19]*I hope in the Lord Jesus to send Timothy to you soon, so that I too may be cheered by news of you.* [20]*For I have no one like him, who will be genuinely concerned for your welfare.* [21]*For they all seek their own interests, not those of Jesus Christ.* [22]*But you know Timothy's proven worth, how as a son with a father he has served with me in the gospel.* [23]*I hope therefore to send him just as soon as I see how it will go with me,* [24]*and I trust in the Lord that shortly I myself will come also.*

FOCUSED THINKING
Notice the journalistic questions (5 W's and 1 H).

1. **Why** does Paul hope to send Timothy to the Philippians?
➤ See 2:19.

2. **What** are Timothy's unique qualities?
➤ See 2:20-22.

PERSONAL APPLICATION
Application demands specific answers to specific questions. Here are two questions to help you apply the truths from *Focused Thinking*:

1. **How** can you increase Timothy's strengths in your life? Be specific.

2. **Who** has proven worth in your life? Be specific.

INTERACTIVE PRAYER
Write a one paragraph prayer for each application.

LIFE JOURNALING
This whole process is journaling. However, this is also a place to record additional thoughts and capture your memories.

Devotional:
Loyalty

Who are the most loyal and loving people in your life? Loyalty is a rare quality in people today. When you look around, who's got your back? Who's there for you in their actions, not just in their words? Is it your spouse? Is it your extended family? Is it your friends?

Who's there for you during the highs and lows of life? Perhaps the most important attribute I need in my family and friends is loyalty. When I have a bad day, I need Karin to be on my side first. I don't need an unbiased opinion; I need a biased opinion. I need someone who fiercely trusts me and believes in me. Why? Because the world is full of people who believe the worst first. I'm not saying I don't want the truth; I'm saying I want trust before I want truth.

What did Paul have in Timothy? He had a young man who trusted Paul even though Paul was in prison. Timothy trusted Paul and was loyal to Paul despite the circumstances. The majority isn't always right; in fact, the majority is rarely right. If truth be told, most people aren't interested in what's right; they are interested in what's right for them.

What was so unique and special about Timothy? Philippians 1:20 says, *"For I have no one like him, who will be genuinely concerned for your welfare."* He had the mind of Christ; in humility he considered others to be more important than himself. He didn't look only to his own interests; he was genuinely concerned for the welfare of others. That's a rare, rare quality. Do you have a Timothy in your life? Do you have more than one? Before you get disappointed about the limited number of them, who considers *you* to be a Timothy in *their* life?

What is the norm with most people? Philippians 1:21 says it this way: *"For they all seek their own interests, not those of Jesus Christ."* The essence of sin is selfishness; therefore, the majority will be *selfish* instead of *selfless*. As a pastor I know a lot of people, but I only have a handful of Timothies. Think about it this way: If I was unjustly thrown in prison, who would stand with me? Who would believe I was innocent until proven guilty? Timothy stood with Paul when all others abandoned him. That's a loyal and loving friend who has proven his worth. It is my hope and prayer that my ministry can produce an army of Timothies.

Read Paul's next statement about Timothy, but listen to it from the perspective of accusations and adversity. *"But you know Timothy's proven worth, how as a son with a father he has served with me in the gospel"* (2:22). Do you see and hear Paul's respect and admiration for Timothy? How much more do you love foxhole buddies? Nothing in life compares to friendships that are forged between soldiers.

If we want loyal and loving friendships, then we must be willing to do two things:

1. Walk with one another through the highs and lows of life.
2. Serve with one another in the advancement of the gospel.

I think the word "loyal" is like the word "love." It's a verb. It's not enough to say you love someone, you have to show it. In the same way, it's not enough to say you're loyal – you must show it. You have to trust people first. You have to care about people's feelings more than the facts. Again, I'm not asking you to compromise; I'm just asking you to be *compassionate*. More times than not, loyalty and love will require you to persevere with people through the messiness of life.

PERSONAL APPLICATION
1. Who are the people who trust you first?
2. Who are the people who persevere with you?
3. Who has your loyalty and love?

Philippians 2:25-30

²⁵I have thought it necessary to send to you Epaphroditus my brother and fellow worker and fellow soldier, and your messenger and minister to my need, ²⁶for he has been longing for you all and has been distressed because you heard that he was ill. ²⁷Indeed he was ill, near to death. But God had mercy on him, and not only on him but on me also, lest I should have sorrow upon sorrow. ²⁸I am the more eager to send him, therefore, that you may rejoice at seeing him again, and that I may be less anxious. ²⁹So receive him in the Lord with all joy, and honor such men, ³⁰for he nearly died for the work of Christ, risking his life to complete what was lacking in your service to me.

FOCUSED THINKING

Notice the journalistic questions (5 W's and 1 H).

1. **How** does Paul describe the strengths and attributes of Epaphroditus?
➤ See 2:25-26, 30.

2. **How** should the church receive Epaphroditus?
➤ See 2:29.

PERSONAL APPLICATION

Application demands specific answers to specific questions. Here are two questions to help you apply the truths from *Focused Thinking*:

1. **How** do you want to be described as a man or woman of God? Be specific.

2. **How** should you receive and treat God's servant leaders? Be specific.

INTERACTIVE PRAYER
Write a one paragraph prayer for each application.

LIFE JOURNALING
This whole process is journaling. However, this is also a place to record additional thoughts and capture your memories.

Devotional:
Honor Your Leaders

None of us like to think about our funerals, but thinking about our death should help us reflect on our life. Think about it this way: What do you want to be said at your funeral? I encourage you to prioritize some time to complete the following five statements:

1. The thing that was most important to me was...
2. People say I stood for...
3. I made a difference in my world by...
4. God was glorified because I...
5. People knew I loved them because...

Those are thought-provoking statements, and they are statements that speak directly to our God-given purpose. Think about these statements in light of Paul's description of Epaphroditus. He called Epaphroditus *"my brother and fellow worker and fellow soldier, and your messenger and minister to my need"* (2:25). Seriously, how could Paul be more honorable? This is the equivalent of a Purple Heart speech for a war hero. When is the last time you wrote a "thank you" card to one of your leaders?

Most leaders are under-appreciated because most people have an incorrect definition of leadership. People think leadership is about rewards; therefore, most people think leaders have everything they need and more. But the reality is this: Leadership isn't about rewards – it is about responsibility. Leaders don't need rewards nearly as much as they need respect, honor and appreciation.

It feels weird and a little self-serving for me to write this since I'm a pastor, but it needs to be said. The next time you go to church, don't just think about what *you* need – think about the needs of your leadership team. Who ministers to the ministers? What was his or her life like this week? How do you minister to others when you've had a terrible week? None of us are exempt from the challenges and crises of life. My son says I should do a documentary called "Six Days to Sunday" for people to really understand the other six days of the week!

Here's the thing about pastoring: It is an emotional roller

coaster. It is a journey that involves all the normal demands of any work environment, but on top of that it is your responsibility to help people to be holy. Hello? It's *not* impossible, but it *feels* impossible. Here's the other interesting and odd dynamic about ministry: When you are successful in ministry, you are actually helping people to see their sin, confess their sin and repent of their sin. Basically, that means ministry is messy. Life is rarely as simple as the three points we teach on Sundays.

What can we learn from Paul's descriptions of Epaphroditus and Timothy (2:19-24)? First and foremost, the life of Christ is more *caught* than it is *taught*. Our greatest need is to experience Christ in and through our leaders. We must experience their faith, hope and love, but the greatest of these is love (1 Corinthians 13:13).

Everything that is modeled and described in these six verses (Philippians 2:25-30) is a picture of love. Paul loved Epaphroditus; Epaphroditus loved the Philippians; and the Philippians loved Paul, Timothy and Epaphroditus. However, it is important to notice that Paul didn't take love for granted. He constantly instructed the Philippians and other churches on *how to receive* God's leaders. In Philippians 2:29, he instructs them to "*receive [Epaphroditus] in the Lord with all joy, and honor such men*." Why was Epaphroditus deserving of honor? Philippians 2:30 says, "*[F]or he nearly died for the work of Christ, risking his life to complete what was lacking in your service to me.*"

PERSONAL APPLICATION

Go back to the first paragraph and complete the five statements that speak about your God-given purpose.

Philippians 3:1-6

¹Finally, my brothers, rejoice in the Lord. To write the same things to you is no trouble to me and is safe for you. ²Look out for the dogs, look out for the evildoers, look out for those who mutilate the flesh. ³For we are the circumcision, who worship by the Spirit of God and glory in Christ Jesus and put no confidence in the flesh— ⁴though I myself have reason for confidence in the flesh also. If anyone else thinks he has reason for confidence in the flesh, I have more: ⁵circumcised on the eighth day, of the people of Israel, of the tribe of Benjamin, a Hebrew of Hebrews; as to the law, a Pharisee; ⁶as to zeal, a persecutor of the church; as to righteousness under the law, blameless.

FOCUSED THINKING

Notice the journalistic questions (5 W's and 1 H).

1. **What** does it mean when Paul says, *"For we are the circumcision"*?
➤ Since this one is not intuitive, be patient; you can find the answer in today's devotional.

2. **How** much confidence should we put in the flesh?
➤ See 3:3.

PERSONAL APPLICATION

Application demands specific answers to specific questions. Here are two questions to help you apply the truths from *Focused Thinking*:

1. **Where** do you unintentionally put confidence in the flesh? Be specific.

2. **Where** should your confidence be? Be specific.

INTERACTIVE PRAYER
Write a one paragraph prayer for each application.

LIFE JOURNALING
This whole process is journaling. However, this is also a place to record additional thoughts and capture your memories.

Devotional:
Intentional Repetition

Why do I repeat the same mistakes over and over again? Why do I have to learn some lessons time and time again?

No doubt you've heard people say that history repeats itself. It's not so much the fact that history repeats itself as it is that sinful nature remains the same throughout history. That's the reason why history repeats itself. Notice what Paul says in 3:1b: "*To write the same things to you is no trouble to me and is safe for you.*" Paul wasn't worried about repetition at all because he knows the persuasive power of the sinful flesh. He knew the issues were much bigger than intellectual solutions.

It's dangerous for us to think we've "got it" because we "know it." Salvation doesn't come from knowing about the death, burial and resurrection of Jesus Christ; it comes from repenting of your sin and placing your faith in Jesus as your Lord and Savior. You have to go beyond information to application. It's critical for us to be reminded that life change doesn't come from *hearing* God's Word; it comes from *obeying* God's Word. The renewing of our mind must lead to the renewing of our desires, decisions and disciplines. It can be summed up in this equation:

Information + Application = Transformation

Do I sound like a broken record? If you've followed my ministry for an extended period of time, how many times have you heard me use that phrase? Here's the reason why I intentionally repeat myself: "*To write the same things to you is no trouble to me and is safe for you.*"

Repetition in itself is also a form of caution, but Paul heightens the warning in 3:2: "*Look out for the dogs, look out for the evildoers, look out for those who mutilate the flesh.*" Paul is warning us against people adding rules, regulations and rituals to our relationship with Jesus. He is telling us to look out for all the ways the enemy attempts to attack us. The enemy has one objective: "*The thief comes only to steal and kill and destroy*" (John 10:10). He wants to steal your joy, kill your relationship with God and destroy your effectiveness for the kingdom. The enemy comes in many different forms with many different voices, but one of the most dangerous is the religious or legalistic voice.

These are the voices that Paul battled given not only his religious history, but also the religious approach of the day and his previous successes as a religious leader.

There is a major difference between religion and relationship. There are many religions and all of them are man's attempt to be right with God. The bible isn't a book about religious people and atheists. The bible is a book about religious people and people who serve the one true God. It is a book about people who honor the first commandment: "*You shall have no other gods before me*" (Exodus 20:3). Relationship is different from religion because it is *God's* way to make man right with God. Many people have said it this way:

- ➤ Religion is spelled *do*.
- ➤ Relationship is spelled *done*.

Now, let's deal with the complex use of the word "circumcision." What in the world does Paul mean when he says, "*For we are the circumcision*" (3:3)? I know this sounds weird today, but circumcision was a sign of the covenant that God made with Abraham, and also became a sign of the Jewish people's allegiance to the Law of Moses as an extension of the promise (covenant) to Abraham. The biggest controversy about circumcision came when the gospel was shared with the Gentiles. Some Jewish believers came to Antioch and taught that the Gentiles had to be circumcised or else they could not be saved (Acts 15:1).

Peter, Barnabas and Paul radically reinterpreted the law of circumcision by keeping the spiritual meaning but rejecting the physical rite. Inspired by the Holy Spirit, they explained that Abraham received the promises by faith *before* circumcision; therefore, the circumcision of the most respected patriarch, although commanded as an everlasting covenant for his physical heirs and extended household, cannot be a requirement for salvation. Paul explained this in his letter to the Galatians. He said it is wrong to view physical circumcision as necessary because that would imply that faith in Christ was not enough (Galatians 5:2).

Paul warned the Philippians about people who were advocates for circumcision: "*Look out for the dogs*" (3:2). He was using Jewish slang for the Gentiles in reference to the Judaizers.

He warned them to *"look out for those who mutilate the flesh"* – a Greek view of the rite of circumcision. Paul emphasizes that the physical rite, at least to the Greek mind, takes away from its spiritual meaning. It is believers who are the true circumcision, all *"who worship by the Spirit of God and glory in Christ Jesus and put no confidence in the flesh"* (3:3). Paul uses his impressive résumé in 3:4-6 to reinforce his bottom line that no one should put confidence in the flesh.

How is it that some commands of the Old Testament are not required today? The best explanation is to understand that the laws are valid in their intent, but changed in their application. For example, laws regarding sacrifice continue to be valid, but we actually obey them through faith in Jesus Christ, who was sacrificed for us. The law required sacrifice, and Jesus confirmed its validity at the same time that he made it unnecessary for us to perform it. The laws are timeless in their purpose, but different in their methods today. This principle influences one of our driving values at Highpoint Church: "We believe timeless truths should be presented in a timely way."

Traditions have their place, but guard against traditions becoming theology. Here are three different ways to say it. But before I repeat myself, let me remind you of what Paul said in 3:1: *"To write the same things to you is no trouble to me and is safe for you."*

1. The theology is timeless; the methods are timely.
2. The substance is timeless; the style is timely.
3. The function is timeless; the form is timely.

This is why Highpoint Church is conservative in its theology, but progressive in its methodology.

PERSONAL APPLICATION
1. What are the repetitive truths of God that you resist?
2. How do you turn that resistance into repentance?

Philippians 3:7-11

[7]But whatever gain I had, I counted as loss for the sake of Christ. [8]Indeed, I count everything as loss because of the surpassing worth of knowing Christ Jesus my Lord. For his sake I have suffered the loss of all things and count them as rubbish, in order that I may gain Christ [9]and be found in him, not having a righteousness of my own that comes from the law, but that which comes through faith in Christ, the righteousness from God that depends on faith— [10]that I may know him and the power of his resurrection, and may share his sufferings, becoming like him in his death, [11]that by any means possible I may attain the resurrection from the dead.

FOCUSED THINKING
Notice the journalistic questions (5 W's and 1 H).

1. **Why** is Paul able to count his past gains as loss?
➤ See 3:7-8.

2. **What** are the things that Paul gains instead of loses?
➤ See 3:8b-11.

PERSONAL APPLICATION
Application demands specific answers to specific questions. Here are two questions to help you apply the truths from *Focused Thinking*:

1. **How** does time change your perspective on gains and losses? Be specific.

2. **What** are the gains in your life right now? Be specific.

INTERACTIVE PRAYER
Write a one paragraph prayer for each application.

LIFE JOURNALING

This whole process is journaling. However, this is also a place to record additional thoughts and capture your memories.

Devotional:
Brutal Honesty

Dive into this counseling appointment with me for a few minutes. This scenario has played out hundreds of times in my twenty years of ministry. Typically, a young man in his twenties comes to me because his life is out of control to one degree or another. The pursuit of pleasure has turned into the problem of pain. I talk to him about his need to repent of sin and place his faith in Christ for the first time, or to repent of sin and return to Christ. Time and time again I've watched people consider the options and say, "I don't know if I can give all that up."

In this moment, it is impossible for me not to smile. I smile because they don't realize the foolishness of their statement. So, I ask them this question: "What is God asking you to give up? Are you here talking to me because of all the pleasure in your life? I didn't think so. Let me ask the question again: 'What is God asking you to give up?' He's asking you to give up all the problems that come from drinking and drugs, all the problems that come from sex outside of marriage, all the problems that come from mismanaging money, and all the problems that come from immaturity."

Why is this such a difficult decision? It is difficult because people typically look at what they are losing instead of what they are gaining. It's almost impossible to repent when you are looking at your sin instead of looking at *the surpassing worth of knowing Christ Jesus my Lord*" (3:8a). Honestly, most of the time the promise of forgiveness alone isn't enough for people to take their eyes off of sin. They need to see the "*surpassing worth of knowing Christ Jesus.*" It is then and only then that they can look at their sin differently.

What is an accurate view of our sin? "*For his sake I have suffered the loss of all things and count them as rubbish, in order that I may gain Christ*" (3:8b). What does the word "rubbish" mean? Do you realize that sometimes bible translators are too proper and dignified in their translations? The bible is not a PG-rated book; it is definitely R-rated. It has to be if it is going to deal with sin in an honest way. The word "rubbish" means bodily excrement. Now, let's translate this verse together: "*For his sake I have suffered the loss of all things and count them as _____, in order that I may gain Christ.*"

Here is Paul's modern day translation of this concept. He is saying, "My heritage and accomplishments are crap compared to the surpassing worth of knowing Christ Jesus my Lord." Are you offended that I'm using the word "crap," or are you offended that you value your "crap" more than knowing Jesus? I know that stings, but it needs to be said. We must not water down the bible for the sake of being proper. There were countless times throughout scripture when Jesus wasn't dignified or proper. How proper was it for Jesus to order Peter, "*Get behind me, Satan!*" (Matthew 16:23)?

What is the secret to counting the cost or suffering the loss of all things? It's important to understand that when the sun comes out, the stars disappear. In other words, when you truly see the brilliance of Christ, the lesser things vanish from view. The secret is to focus on what you are gaining instead of losing. Let me illustrate it in a more romantic way: On my wedding day, was I focused on what I was gaining or losing? Suffice it to say, I wasn't looking at other women when my bride was walking down the aisle!

No one suffers loss for a set of rules and rituals, but we are willing to suffer loss for a relationship. Paul says, "*Indeed, I count everything as **loss** because of the **surpassing worth** of knowing Christ Jesus my Lord. For his sake, I have suffered the **loss of all things** and count them as **rubbish**, in order that I **may gain Christ**" (3:8).

It's time to be brutally honest about the choice before us; it's time to choose Christ over crap. Everything in this life is "bodily excrement" apart from the surpassing worth of knowing Christ Jesus. Your righteousness is crap compared with His righteousness. Christianity isn't an add-on to your life. It isn't just the repentance of your sin; it is the repentance of your righteousness. What happens when you count everything as rubbish? You may "*be found in him, not having a righteousness of [your] own that comes from the law, but that which comes through faith in Christ, the righteousness from God that depends on faith*" (3:9).

What do you gain when you choose Christ?

➤ You gain the righteousness from God that depends on faith (3:9).
➤ You gain knowing Him and the power of His resurrection (3:10).
➤ You gain sharing in His sufferings (3:10).
➤ You gain attaining resurrection from the dead (3:11).

PERSONAL APPLICATION

1. What are you afraid of losing?
2. Why are you afraid of losing crap?
3. What do you need to do to shift your focus from losing to gaining?

Philippians 3:12-16

¹²Not that I have already obtained this or am already perfect, but I press on to make it my own, because Christ Jesus has made me his own. ¹³Brothers, I do not consider that I have made it my own. But one thing I do: forgetting what lies behind and straining forward to what lies ahead, ¹⁴I press on toward the goal for the prize of the upward call of God in Christ Jesus. ¹⁵Let those of us who are mature think this way, and if in anything you think otherwise, God will reveal that also to you. ¹⁶Only let us hold true to what we have attained.

FOCUSED THINKING
Notice the journalistic questions (5 W's and 1 H).

1. **What** is the one thing Paul does?
➤ See 3:13-14.

2. **What** is Paul's motivation?
➤ See 3:14.

PERSONAL APPLICATION
Application demands specific answers to specific questions. Here are two questions to help you apply the truths from *Focused Thinking*:

1. **What** do you need to do to narrow your focus on one thing? Be specific.

2. **What** adjustments do you need to make to press on toward the goal? Be specific.

INTERACTIVE PRAYER
Write a one paragraph prayer for each application.

LIFE JOURNALING

This whole process is journaling. However, this is also a place to record additional thoughts and capture your memories.

Devotional:
Relentless Focus

How do you respond to the statement, "I dare you"? For good or bad, I'm a sucker for a challenge. There is something about that statement that makes me feel alive. I rarely ask the question, "What if it doesn't work?" I typically ask the question, "What if it *does* work?"

The answer to that question is how a vision is born. A vision is a clear mental picture of what could be, fueled by the conviction that it *should* be. A vision forms in the hearts of those who are dissatisfied with the status quo. What are you dissatisfied with in your life? What is God's vision for your life? What is God's vision for the church?

Over twenty years ago, God dared me to do one thing: To "*[forget] what lies behind and [strain] forward to what lies ahead*" (3:13). It was during my junior year in college when I decided to replace my goals with God's goals. My goal was to play professional golf. There was nothing wrong with my goal; the problem was me. I was looking to golf to meet all of my needs and desires. Golf was my idol and I served it well.

However, my life didn't change simply because I quit pursuing golf. My life changed because "*I [pressed] on toward the goal for the prize of the upward call of God in Christ Jesus*" (3:14). God's goal became the driving force in my life. It began with the desire to know Him, but it quickly expanded to the desire to make Him known. A few short years later God did the unexpected – He called me to the ministry and gave me a vision for starting a church. In this moment God dared me to "destroy the box" – the church box. He dared me to start Highpoint Church: A perfect place for imperfect people. A place where people see Jesus as the Friend of Sinners. A place where people receive compassion without compromise. A people who live to prove that love works. Ultimately, a welcoming place for people who are turning to God (Acts 15:19).

God used these verses in Philippians 3:12-16 to give me a vision for dismantling apathy. God didn't design us for apathy, and He definitely didn't die for us to be apathetic. Apathy is a lack of feeling or emotion or interest. How can we be apathetic when we are commanded to love God with *all* our heart, *all* our soul, *all* our mind and *all* our strength?

Notice how Paul describes the pursuit of the prize: "*Not that I have already obtained this or am already perfect, but I press on to make it my own*" (3:12). I love that mentality; Paul wasn't apathetic, he was relentless. He was relentless about "*[pressing] on toward the goal for the prize of the upward call of God in Christ Jesus*" (3:14). In many respects, it would be fair to say that "to press on" is to be relentlessly focused. Paul was focused on knowing Him and making Him known. The secret to focus is the process of elimination. He eliminated everything that competed with his focus on Christ. It's important to remember that a lack of focus always leads to a lack of results.

How do you know if you are pressing on? It's a ridiculous question. If you don't know then you aren't doing it. It's time to increase your spiritual intensity. Jesus never told us to play it safe. History teaches over and over again that it doesn't take a lot of people to change the world; it just takes a few who are "*[pressing] on toward the goal for the prize of the upward call of God in Christ Jesus*" (3:14).

John Wesley said it this way: "Give me ten men who hate nothing but sin and love nothing but God, and we'll change the world."

PERSONAL APPLICATION

1. What competes with God's goals in your life?
2. What do you need to eliminate in order to be relentlessly focused?

Philippians 3:17-21

[17]*Brothers, join in imitating me, and keep your eyes on those who walk according to the example you have in us.* [18]*For many, of whom I have often told you and now tell you even with tears, walk as enemies of the cross of Christ.* [19]*Their end is destruction, their god is their belly, and they glory in their shame, with minds set on earthly things.* [20]*But our citizenship is in heaven, and from it we await a Savior, the Lord Jesus Christ,* [21]*who will transform our lowly body to be like his glorious body, by the power that enables him even to subject all things to himself.*

FOCUSED THINKING

Notice the journalistic questions (5 W's and 1 H).

1. **What** is the difference between leaders who are good examples and leaders who are bad examples?
➤ See 3:18-21.

2. **What** are the promises that await us in heaven?
➤ See 3:20-21.

PERSONAL APPLICATION

Application demands specific answers to specific questions. Here are two questions to help you apply the truths from *Focused Thinking*:

1. **What** do you need to imitate from your church leaders today? Be specific.

2. **How** can we prioritize transformation on this side of heaven? Be specific.

INTERACTIVE PRAYER

Write a one paragraph prayer for each application.

LIFE JOURNALING

This whole process is journaling. However, this is also a place to record additional thoughts and capture your memories.

Devotional:
The Leader's Focus

Do you ever play the comparison game? Of course you do; everyone does it. All of us are constantly comparing ourselves with others to see if we measure up. Are we better than our peers, equal with our peers or behind our peers? The comparison *game* is ultimately the comparison *trap,* because good is never good enough. There's always someone better, someone prettier, someone smarter, someone more successful.

What if you didn't have to play that game anymore? What if comparison could be positive instead of negative? In God's economy of leadership you don't have to step on your friends on your way up the ladder. In fact, God flips leadership upside down and makes it about serving instead of being served.

Notice how Paul is inviting people to imitate him as a leader: *"Brothers, join in imitating me, and keep your eyes on those who walk according to the example you have in us"* (3:17). He isn't trying to protect his intellectual capital. He is sharing his trade secrets for the purpose of equipping more leaders. Paul understood that there is no success without a successor.

What qualities of leadership did Paul, Timothy and Epaphroditus model throughout Philippians? They've modeled humble leadership. It hasn't been about them; it's been about the glory of God and the good of people. They've prayed for people, served people and sacrificed for people. They've modeled leadership that is focused and goal-driven. Unfortunately, that's not the case with the majority of leadership then or now. *"For many, of whom I have often told you and now tell you even with tears, walk as enemies of the cross of Christ. Their end is destruction, their god is their belly, and they glory in their shame, with minds set on earthly things"* (3:18-19).

This has to be the defining difference between godly and ungodly leadership: *"[W]ith their minds set on earthly things."* Do you remember what Jesus said to Peter after he said, *"Get behind me, Satan!"*? He went on to say, *"You are a hindrance to me. For you are not setting your mind on the things of God, but on the things of man"* (Matthew 16:23). Your focus is the difference. Everything is driven by the direction of your focus: Heaven or earth; Jesus or you. Once again, we must return to this truth: Leadership isn't about rewards; it is about responsibility. It is the leaders' responsibility to set their *"minds on things that are above, not on things that are on earth"* (Colossians 3:2).

Why is this the defining difference? Philippians 3:20-21 says it this way: *"But our citizenship is in heaven, and from it we await a Savior, the Lord Jesus Christ, who will transform our lowly body to be like his glorious body, by the power that enables him even to subject all things to himself."* It is critical for us to understand that *this* life is an opportunity to invest in *that* life. What we invest here determines what we receive there. Additionally, the more we live for the next world, the better this world will be.

Do you have this perspective yet? God doesn't promise that heaven is a place of equal rewards, roles and responsibilities. In fact, it is quite the opposite. He promises that our stewardship here will influence our leadership there. The focus of your life and leadership determines your rewards in heaven.

PERSONAL APPLICATION

What would you do differently if you truly believed God *"rewards those who seek Him"* (Hebrews 11:6)?

Notice the focus on rewards in these scriptural examples:

2 Corinthians 5:10
*For we must all appear before the judgment seat of Christ, so that **each one may receive what is due for what he has done in the body**, whether good or evil.*

Colossians 3:23-24
*Whatever you do, **work heartily**, as for the Lord and not for men, **knowing that from the Lord you will receive the inheritance as your reward**. You are serving the Lord Christ.*

Hebrews 11:6
*And without faith it is impossible to please him, for whoever would draw near to God **must believe that he exists** and that **he rewards those who seek him**.*

Philippians 4:1-3
¹Therefore, my brothers, whom I love and long for, my joy and crown, stand firm thus in the Lord, my beloved.
²I entreat Euodia and I entreat Syntyche to agree in the Lord.
³Yes, I ask you also, true companion, help these women, who have labored side by side with me in the gospel together with Clement and the rest of my fellow workers, whose names are in the book of life.

FOCUSED THINKING
Notice the journalistic questions (5 W's and 1 H).

1. **How** does Paul describe his brothers?
➤ See 4:1.

2. **How** does Paul address unity problems in the body?
➤ See 4:2-3.

PERSONAL APPLICATION
Application demands specific answers to specific questions. Here are two questions to help you apply the truths from *Focused Thinking*:

1. **Who** do you feel so deeply about and why? Be specific.

2. **How** can you help solve unity problems today? Be specific.

INTERACTIVE PRAYER
Write a one paragraph prayer for each application.

LIFE JOURNALING
This whole process is journaling. However, this is also a place to record additional thoughts and capture your memories.

Devotional:
Problem Solving

What do you worry about? Most people worry about succeeding in their careers, being secure in their finances or being strong in their relationships. I can survive adversity in a lot of areas, but it stresses me out when my relationships are struggling. Think about it this way: As a pastor, Paul was a spiritual parent to all of his churches. Just as parents are always concerned about the relationships between siblings, pastors are always concerned about the unity of the church. Nothing hurts a family or church more than a lack of unity.

Listen to Paul's heart for his people in Philippians 4:1: "*Therefore, my brothers, whom I love and long for, my joy and crown, stand firm thus in the Lord, my beloved.*" Don't run too fast past the relational depth of the phrases "*whom I love and long for*" and "*my joy and crown.*" Think about this for a moment: Whom can you speak this highly about?

Paul defined his success by the success of his followers. His greatest success was for his followers to be known by love. The stronger love and unity is in the body, the easier it is to spot a *lack* of love and unity in the body. Unfortunately, it is difficult for us to fully comprehend Paul's passion for unity because this level of relationship isn't the norm in American churches.

The enemy understands the importance of unity and relentlessly attacks it. This is why Paul tells the Philippians to "*stand firm*" in the Lord (4:1). To "stand firm" means to stand unmoved against the enemy. Paul instructs us to stand firm by following his example (3:17), by focusing on heaven instead of earth (3:19-21), and by living in harmony with one another (4:2).

Unity is so important that Paul addresses the problem – and people – specifically. In 4:2-3, notice how he called upon the church to address and solve this problem: "*I entreat Euodia and I entreat Syntyche to agree in the Lord. Yes, I ask you also, true companion, help these women, who have labored side by side with me in the gospel together with Clement and the rest of my fellow workers, whose names are in the book of life.*"

The problem was *divisive* enough that the Philippians wrote to Paul about it, and *big* enough that Paul assigned a mediator to it. Notice that Paul didn't discredit Euodia and Syntyche; he chose to refocus them. He shifted their focus to their citizenship in heaven, reminding them that their *"names are in the book of life"* (4:3).

PERSONAL APPLICATION

1. What relationships in your life need to be reconciled?
2. What do you need to do to move toward reconciliation?

Philippians 4:4-7

⁴Rejoice in the Lord always; again I will say, rejoice. ⁵Let your reasonableness be known to everyone. The Lord is at hand; ⁶do not be anxious about anything, but in everything by prayer and supplication with thanksgiving let your requests be made known to God. ⁷And the peace of God, which surpasses all understanding, will guard your hearts and your minds in Christ Jesus.

FOCUSED THINKING

Notice the journalistic questions (5 W's and 1 H).

1. **How** should we overcome problems?
➤ See 4:4-6.

2. **What** is the relationship between prayer and peace?
➤ See 4:6-7.

PERSONAL APPLICATION

Application demands specific answers to specific questions. Here are two questions to help you apply the truths from *Focused Thinking*:

1. **What** should be the primary expressions of our attitude in problem solving? Be specific.

2. **When** have you experienced peace in the midst of problems? Be specific.

INTERACTIVE PRAYER

Write a one paragraph prayer for each application.

LIFE JOURNALING

This whole process is journaling. However, this is also a place to record additional thoughts and capture your memories.

Devotional:
The Reality of Rejoicing

What memories do you associate with rejoicing? First of all, I never remember rejoicing alone. I tend to think about accomplishments in the context of teams. I think about celebrating with my teammates, my family and my friends. I remember specific ceremonies like marriage, graduations and anniversaries. I focus on the accomplishments of my wife, my kids and my peers. Now that I think about it, I rejoice the most on vacations! They give me an opportunity to slow down enough to reflect and rejoice.

Back to our text, that's not the specific context for Paul's words on rejoicing here. He says, *"Rejoice in the Lord always; again I will say, rejoice"* (4:4). Wait a second - he said "always." Honestly, "always" isn't realistic or possible. Not only that, but in the first four verses of this chapter, Paul addressed the problem of disunity between Euodia and Syntyche!

However, it's possible to rejoice in the midst of adversity because we are commanded to rejoice in the Lord, *not* in circumstances. We aren't victims of our circumstances. It's important to remember that *my* response is *my* responsibility. My attitude is a choice. It's a choice to believe instead of doubt. It's a choice to persevere instead of quit. An attitude of rejoicing causes you to approach adversity with confidence and control. It enables you to focus on the solution instead of the problem.

Notice how Paul instructs the Philippians in problem solving: *"Let your reasonableness be known to everyone. The Lord is at hand; do not be anxious about anything, but in everything by prayer and supplication with thanksgiving let your requests be made known to God"* (4:5-6).

An attitude of rejoicing makes it much easier to be reasonable to everyone. How reasonable are you when you're anxious or angry? Have you ever noticed that the madder you get, the dumber you get? I love what Paul says next: *"The Lord is at hand"* (3:5b). This is a strong reminder that Jesus is sovereign and in control. His presence stabilizes everything, even in the midst of instability. God's presence is the key to moving from problems to peace.

Paul instructs us to replace anxiety with prayer. If I'm honest, I'm still anxious when I pray; but I'm less anxious. However, there are times when the anxiety is replaced with peace, confidence and even boldness. Few things can comprehensively change my disposition like prayer. It is through rejoicing, reasonableness and prayer that we experience the peace of God regardless of our circumstances. All of these things come together and result in the ultimate promise in Philippians 4:7. It says, *"And the peace of God, which surpasses all understanding, will guard your hearts and your minds in Christ Jesus."*

PERSONAL APPLICATION

1. What is the biggest problem you are facing right now?
2. What do you need to do to move from *problem* to *peace*?

Philippians 4:8-9

8Finally, brothers, whatever is true, whatever is honorable, whatever is just, whatever is pure, whatever is lovely, whatever is commendable, if there is any excellence, if there is anything worthy of praise, think about these things. 9What you have learned and received and heard and seen in me—practice these things, and the God of peace will be with you.

FOCUSED THINKING

Notice the journalistic questions (5 W's and 1 H).

1. **What** should we think about?
➤ See 4:8.

2. **What** should we practice?
➤ See 4:9.

PERSONAL APPLICATION

Application demands specific answers to specific questions. Here are two questions to help you apply the truths from *Focused Thinking*:

1. **What** are the top three ways you can discipline yourself to think about these things? Be specific.

2. **Who** are the top three people in your circle of influence that you need to learn from? Be specific.

INTERACTIVE PRAYER

Write a one paragraph prayer for each application.

LIFE JOURNALING

This whole process is journaling. However, this is also a place to record additional thoughts and capture your memories.

Devotional:
Fulfill Your Potential

How do we fulfill our divine potential? God didn't create any of us to be average. It's my responsibility to be the best me that I can. I don't have to be better than anyone else; I simply have to be a good steward of being me. No one can be as good at being me as me. I'm one of a kind for God's glory and man's good. I don't have to prove myself through performance, but I do have the opportunity to maximize my strengths and minimize my weaknesses.

Potential isn't just a term or concept that's associated with sports. All of us have potential for good or bad, but ultimately, that is determined by our relationship with Jesus Christ. When we discover our God-given passions, power and purpose, we have unlimited potential.

Let me give you a biblical foundation for God's commitment to developing your divine potential.

> ➤ *Potential begins* with God's declaration that His plans are to give you a future and a hope (Jeremiah 29:11).
> ➤ *Potential is possible* because His divine power has granted to you all things that pertain to life and godliness (2 Peter 1:3-11).
> ➤ *Potential is developed* when you think on these things and practice these things (Philippians 4:8-9).
> ➤ *Potential is experienced* when you walk by the Spirit and bear the fruit of the Spirit (Galatians 5:16, 22-24).
> ➤ *Potential is fulfilled* when God does far more abundantly than all that you ask or think, according to the power at work within you (Ephesians 3:20).

Potential is the place where the things we love to do and the things we are good at come together. There are few things in life as powerful as aligning your passions, strengths and goals. Don't make this too complicated; it should be obvious where you do and don't have potential. It's really a simple three-step process:

1. Eliminate the obvious. (I can't sing.)
2. Identify the obvious. (I can lead and teach.)
3. Do the obvious. (I'm the Lead Pastor at Highpoint Church.)

What does your potential look like spiritually? You will never fulfill your potential as a man or woman of God until you act on Jesus' resurrection power in your life. It's important to understand that potential becomes power when you abide in Jesus, walk by His Spirit, and renew your mind with His Word. Philippians 4:8-9 emphasizes the importance of renewing our minds by instructing us to "*think about these things*" and "*practice these things*."

Renewing our minds with the Word is one of the ways in which we "*think about these things*," but we also do it by valuing what God values. People of God should discipline themselves to focus on "*whatever is true, whatever is honorable, whatever is just, whatever is pure, whatever is lovely, whatever is commendable, if there is any excellence, if there is anything worthy of praise*" (4:8). How would that approach to life change your attitude? Focus is the process of elimination; you are eliminating the negative and focusing on the positive. It's never too early or too late to run toward your God-given potential. God promises us that He will redeem our past. God is a good steward of our past.

It's important to remember that godliness takes time. My mentor, Clyde Cranford, often said, "Once you have spiritual disciplines, God grows you as fast as He can without killing you." This is a good time to remind you that it takes time to go through the following physical and spiritual progression: from babes to children, from children to young men, from young men to men, from men to fathers, from father to elders, and from elders to aged.

Who do you respect and admire as a leader? Philippians 4:9 says, "*What you have learned and received and heard and seen in me—practice these things.*" It's vitally important to understand that you can't have their prize without the practice. You must discipline yourself to learn and receive from them. You must watch them, listen to them and practice what you see in them. These leaders make the results look easy; but that is far from the truth. They've spent a lifetime developing their potential. You aren't experiencing their *potential*; you are experiencing their *results*. This is one of the many reasons why sustained success is more impressive than instant success.

What are the results of "*thinking about these things*" and "*practicing these things*"? "*[P]ractice these things, and the God of peace will be with you*" (4:9). That's a remarkable promise! Notice that he didn't say, "... and the **peace of God** will be with you." Rather, he said, "... *and the **God of peace** will be with you*." That's a difference maker; that's much more than peaceful circumstances.

Are you fulfilling your God-given potential? If not, why not? People rarely fail; they usually give up. Whatever you do, don't give up.

PERSONAL APPLICATION

1. Why have you given up before?
2. What's going to be different this time?

Philippians 4:10-13

¹⁰I rejoiced in the Lord greatly that now at length you have revived your concern for me. You were indeed concerned for me, but you had no opportunity. ¹¹Not that I am speaking of being in need, for I have learned in whatever situation I am to be content. ¹²I know how to be brought low, and I know how to abound. In any and every circumstance, I have learned the secret of facing plenty and hunger, abundance and need. ¹³I can do all things through him who strengthens me.

FOCUSED THINKING

Notice the journalistic questions (5 W's and 1 H).

1. **What** has Paul learned, regardless of his situation?
➤ See 4:11-12.

2. **What** could Paul do through Christ?
➤ See 4:13.

PERSONAL APPLICATION

Application demands specific answers to specific questions. Here are two questions to help you apply the truths from *Focused Thinking*:

1. **What** have you learned about being content? Be specific.

2. **What** is God calling you to accomplish through His strength? Be specific.

INTERACTIVE PRAYER

Write a one paragraph prayer for each application.

LIFE JOURNALING

This whole process is journaling. However, this is also a place to record additional thoughts and capture your memories.

Devotional:
Discontent or Content?

How do you define happiness? Most people define happiness circumstantially. If circumstances are good then I'm happy; if not, then I'm unhappy. How happy can you be if you define happiness by circumstances? In a normal week, how many days are good circumstantially? This is sad, but sometimes I find myself surprised when I or others describe a day as "good." Are 50% of your days good circumstantially? That's 3.5 days a week, 15 days a month, and 182.5 days a year. Are you content with life being 50% good and 50% bad? When I dream about life, I don't dream about it only being half good.

If you define life by circumstances, then you'll probably be more unhappy than happy. When circumstances are good, they are rarely good enough. Yet when circumstances are bad, they can always get worse. It is easier for circumstances to be discouraging than it is for them to be encouraging.

If all of this is true, how does Paul continue to talk about rejoicing throughout this chapter of Philippians? First he said, *"Rejoice in the Lord always; again I will say, rejoice"* (4:4). Now he says, *"I rejoiced in the Lord greatly that now at length you have revived your concern for me"* (4:10). Once again, rejoicing rises above circumstances and involves relationships. In the first instance, Paul was solving a problem of disunity; this time he is thanking the people for investing in his ministry.

There is a deep and profound relationship between *rejoicing* and *contentment*. I think Paul's ability to rejoice is founded in his contentment. Notice how contentment doesn't depend upon circumstances; rather, it is remaining calm and confident *through* circumstances. It is the peace that passes all understanding, regardless of the circumstances.

It's hard to see the true value of contentment without defining the difference between *discontentment* and *contentment*. Discontentment focuses on what I don't have, while contentment focuses on what I do have. Discontentment is living from a spirit of greed. It's the equivalent of saying I'm discontent because I don't have the circumstances I want. I'm discontent because I don't have the marriage I want, the job I want or the money I want. Have you noticed that it is easier to be discontent than content?

If discontentment is living from a spirit of greed, then contentment is living from a spirit of gratitude. I'm content when I'm grateful that *"the Lord is at hand"* (4:5) and when the *"God of peace"* (4:9) is with me. I'm content when I'm *"thinking about these things"* and *"practicing these things"* (4:8-9). Lastly, I'm content when I expect less from circumstances and more from Christ (4:10-13).

Do you see how contentment doesn't depend on circumstances? Paul couldn't be more clear about this. Here's the bottom line: Contentment isn't about having more or less; it's about having Christ. However, let's not be so spiritual that we're unrealistic. Contentment doesn't mean you are happy with your circumstances. You don't have to deny your disappointments, feelings and preferences in order to be content. This is why Paul says, *"I can do all things through him who strengthens me"* (4:13). In this way, contentment is accessing His strength to persevere and press on.

PERSONAL APPLICATION

1. Where are you discontent right now?
2. Why are you discontent?
3. What do you need to do to replace discontentment with contentment?

Philippians 4:14-23

14Yet it was kind of you to share my trouble. 15And you Philippians yourselves know that in the beginning of the gospel, when I left Macedonia, no church entered into partnership with me in giving and receiving, except you only. 16Even in Thessalonica you sent me help for my needs once and again. 17Not that I seek the gift, but I seek the fruit that increases to your credit. 18I have received full payment, and more. I am well supplied, having received from Epaphroditus the gifts you sent, a fragrant offering, a sacrifice acceptable and pleasing to God. 19And my God will supply every need of yours according to his riches in glory in Christ Jesus. 20To our God and Father be glory forever and ever. Amen.
21Greet every saint in Christ Jesus. The brothers who are with me greet you. 22All the saints greet you, especially those of Caesar's household.
23The grace of the Lord Jesus Christ be with your spirit.

FOCUSED THINKING

Notice the journalistic questions (5 W's and 1 H).

1. **How** did the Philippians partner with Paul?
➤ See 4:15-16.

2. **What** does Paul seek for the Philippians?
➤ See 4:17.

PERSONAL APPLICATION

Application demands specific answers to specific questions. Here are two questions to help you apply the truths from *Focused Thinking*:

1. **How** do you need to partner with your church today? Be specific.

2. **How** does God meet your needs as a giver? Be specific.

INTERACTIVE PRAYER

Write a one paragraph prayer for each application.

LIFE JOURNALING

This whole process is journaling. However, this is also a place to record additional thoughts and capture your memories.

Devotional:
Minimum or Maximum?

Have you ever been in financial need? Has someone ever given sacrificially to meet your need? Few things generate love, respect and appreciation more than someone giving to you financially. All of us understand that level of appreciation because all of us struggle with our own love of money. We know people are saying "no" to themselves in order to say "yes" to us. If that's not significant enough, our gratitude swells off the charts when we realize no one else was willing to give.

I remember this type of situation well from when we first started Highpoint Church. I visited over thirty pastors and casted our vision and requested their participation in the gospel. Only two responded positively, and I'll never forget those two. They have a special place in my heart over a decade later. One is Colonial Hills Church in Southaven, MS, and the other is a church we recently adopted and turned into the Highpoint Collierville Campus. It's amazing how strong that bond is today. It's important to never forget the people who have helped you along the way.

I find Paul's wording insightful: "*Yet it was kind of you to share my trouble*" (4:14). When people help us with our financial needs, they are "sharing" or "shouldering" our trouble. They are helping us lift the weight. Everyone wanted to be blessed by Paul's ministry, but not everyone wanted to bless Paul's ministry. Look at Philippians 4:15. It says, "*And you Philippians yourselves know that in the beginning of the gospel, when I left Macedonia, no church entered into partnership with me in giving and receiving, except you only.*"

The people of Philippi knew that giving isn't a matter of convenience but of conviction. They believed in Paul, his message and his mission; therefore, they had a conviction to give. They also understood that it was giving and receiving, not just giving. The other churches received but had not given. Receiving should lead to giving, not just more receiving. What do you typically think of people who are receivers only? Are you a giver *and* receiver, or are you a receiver only?

Not only is giving a matter of conviction, but it is also a matter of commitment. They didn't just give once, they gave consistently. "*Even in Thessalonica you sent me help for my needs once and again*" (4:16). Nowadays, giving can be as easy as the click of a button, but in their day giving required intentionality. It looks like they prioritized consistent giving. Nothing is more helpful from a ministry perspective because it enables the leaders to plan strategically.

How did Paul respond to their giving? Philippians 4:17 says, "*Not that I seek the gift, but I seek the fruit that increases to your credit.*" Paul's response is perfect, especially given the number of pastors who haven't been above reproach in this area. Since Paul had learned to be content regardless of his circumstances, he was able to focus on *their* profit instead of *his* profit. Paul was content with circumstances, but he wasn't content in ministry. He wanted believers to grow and the gospel to advance.

Ultimately, giving is an expression of worship that generates gratitude from all. Philippians 4:18-20 says it this way: "*I have received full payment, and more. I am well supplied, having received from Epaphroditus the gifts you sent, a fragrant offering, a sacrifice acceptable and pleasing to God. And my God will supply every need of yours according to his riches in glory in Christ Jesus. To our God and Father be glory forever and ever. Amen.*"

The Philippians were unique as givers. They didn't ask, "How little can I give to keep God happy?" They understood the difference between giving the minimum and giving the maximum. Since they saw giving as an expression of worship, they knew minimal giving wasn't "*a fragrant offering, a sacrifice acceptable and pleasing to God*" (4:18). It's time to change our perspective about giving. It shouldn't be negative. It's only negative because we love money so much; instead, we must replace the love of money with the love of mission.

PERSONAL APPLICATION

1. How much would worship increase if we gave our first 10%?
2. How much would ministry and mission increase if we gave our first 10%?
3. Do you give your first 10%? If not, why not?

Appendix A
FREQUENTLY ASKED QUESTIONS

1. WHY DON'T PEOPLE HAVE A PRIORITY TIME?

They don't trust the reliability of the bible.

People are always trying to attack the reliability of the bible, but it continues to stand the test of time. Forty different writers wrote during a period of 1,600 years and produced the most historically reliable, respected and resilient book in the world. The book may be debated, but it has never been defeated. Historical, archeological and scientific discoveries are constantly confirming the reliability and authority of the bible. If you have questions about the reliability of the bible, I recommend the following resources: *Can I Trust the Bible?* by Darrell L. Dock, *The Apologetics Study Bible* by Ted Cabal and *The New Evidence That Demands a Verdict* by Josh McDowell.

They don't think the bible is relevant.

People question the bible's relevance, but the more we understand our history, the more relevant the bible becomes. History repeats itself because man's sinful nature remains the same throughout history. The bible is relevant because it speaks to the sinful nature – it speaks to our imperfection.

The lack of relevance isn't a biblical issue; it is a presentation issue. The bible isn't a textbook. It is an R-rated, high-definition, digital-sound movie full of love and tragedy, heroes and villains, victories and defeats. It is the greatest story ever told.

The relevance of the bible depends on three questions:

➤ What did it mean to the original hearers?
➤ What is the underlying timeless truth?
➤ How can I practice that truth?

They don't know how to read the bible.

People read whatever they want to or need to. They read for education, development and pleasure. They don't have a reading problem; they have a motivation problem. Do you read your text messages? What if God sent you a text message? Would you say, "I don't know how to read it"? God has sent you countless "text messages." Essentially, this study is teaching you how to open your bible app and read His Word.

They don't have time to read the bible.

Yes, people are busy. But all of us make time for our priorities, pursuits and pleasures. Reading the bible isn't a time issue; it's a priority issue. How much time do people spend on social media or watching television?

I believe that reading the bible is the one priority that determines all others. When I read, apply and pray God's Word, I am putting God first in every area of my life. I believe the Creator of time gives us enough time to have a priority time!

They don't know the benefits of reading the bible.

Let me be clear. I don't want to guilt people into reading the bible; I want to inspire them. Guilt is a poor motivator, and it is always temporary.

What are the benefits of reading the bible? The Word of God is the key to knowing the God of the Word. The common denominator of every great man and woman of God throughout history is that they spent time in the Word and in prayer. Our ability to believe and obey the Word is the difference between faith and faithlessness, hope and hopelessness, love and emptiness. The Word of God is the foundation of transformation.

2. WHERE DO I START? HOW DO I DETERMINE WHAT TO READ?

First, go through the gospel of John.

Return to the gospels frequently because they capture the life and teachings of Jesus Christ.

Second, rotate between the Old Testament and New Testament.

If you have not read through the bible systematically, I'd start with Matthew, rotate to Genesis, move to Mark, rotate to Exodus and so forth. You are simply following the table of contents between the Old and New Testaments.

The only exceptions would be reading the following books together before you rotate to the Old Testament: 1st and 2nd Corinthians; 1st and 2nd Thessalonians; 1st and 2nd Timothy; 1st and 2nd Peter; and 1st, 2nd and 3rd John.

Recommended Resource: *The Chronological Study Bible* by Thomas Nelson.

3. WHEN SHOULD I HAVE MY PRIORITY TIME?

Mark 1:35
In the early morning, while it was still dark, Jesus got up, left the house and went away to a secluded place and was praying there.

Psalm 5:3
In the morning, O LORD, You will hear my voice; in the morning I will order my prayer to You and eagerly watch.

The morning was the pattern of Jesus. The morning sets your heart and mind on God and His will for the day. The morning demonstrates that God is the first priority in your life.
- ➤ Pick a specific start time.
- ➤ Pick a specific amount of time. (Start small and build.)

4. WHERE SHOULD I HAVE MY PRIORITY TIME?

Luke 22:39
And He came out and proceeded as was His custom to the Mount of Olives; and the disciples also followed Him.

Find a place that promotes good study habits.
- ➤ Where you can give God your undivided attention.
- ➤ Where you can pray out loud.
- ➤ Where you can be vulnerable before God.

5. HOW LONG SHOULD MY PRIORITY TIME LAST?

Start with fifteen minutes, and let it grow from there.
- ➤ Initially, it is better to be consistent than it is to be lengthy.
- ➤ As a point of comparison, after twenty years of priority times, mine are typically between thirty and sixty minutes.

6. HOW DO I OVERCOME THE PROBLEM OF DISCIPLINE?

The problem of discipline
Discipline is not your problem; motivation is your problem.
- If you have motivation, discipline is no problem.
- If you lack motivation, discipline is a problem.
- If you approach the problem by saying, "I've got to be more disciplined," you will continually struggle.
- If you find the proper motivation for the problem, your motivation will lead to discipline.

Suggestions
- Your motivation should be love and life change.
- Discipline is delayed gratification.
- The key to discipline is advanced decision making.

7. HOW DO I OVERCOME THE PROBLEM OF DISTRACTIONS?

The problem of distractions
- Is your time consistent?
- Is your environment consistent and distraction-free?
- Are you stuck in your methods or just going through the motions?

Suggestions
Time:
- Pick a specific start time and amount of time Monday through Friday.
  - Example: Monday – Friday from 6:30 – 7:00 a.m.
  - Weekend example: Adjustable but still keep it in the morning.
    - Most people have fewer distractions in the morning. I recommend you reduce or eliminate early-morning appointments because you already have one each morning with God.

Environment:
- Pick a consistent environment for your priority time.
  - A room where you can shut the door if needed.

➢ A room with a quality study space (desk, chair, etc.).

➢ A room where you can kneel or lay face down to pray.

Methods:

➤ If you normally start with the Word, change it up and start with prayer. If you start with prayer, change it up and start with the Word.

➤ If you can sing or play music, sing to God. If you can't sing, put on headphones and sing anyway!

➤ If you are stuck in a book, change books.

➤ When you are battling distractions, I recommend evaluating the strengths and weaknesses of your priority time and setting new goals.

➢ Write out one specific application each day.

➢ Determine the most important application for the week.

➢ Write out a prayer each day.

➢ Slow down and focus on quality instead of quantity.

➢ Be mentored, or mentor someone, in a priority time weekly, bi-weekly or monthly.

8. HOW DO I OVERCOME THE PROBLEM OF DISCOURAGEMENT?

The problem of discouragement

➤ Are you struggling in your relationship with God or with others?

➤ Are you struggling to experience a life change?

➤ Are you struggling with sin/strongholds?

Suggestions

Refocus on worship.

➤ Your priority is to fear (stand in awe of) God.

➤ Your priority is to bow down to God.

➤ Your priority is to serve God.

Refocus on spirit and truth, not just truth. Ask the Holy Spirit to:

➤ Fill you up with all the fullness of God. (Ephesians 3:19)

➤ Convict you of sin, righteousness and judgment. (John 16:8)

➤ Guide you into all truth. (John 16:13-15)

➤ Reveal to you what is to come. (John 16:13-15)

➤ Glorify Jesus and reveal Himself to you. (John 16:13-15)

➤ Answer your prayers so that your joy may be made full. (John 16:23-24)

Refocus on thanksgiving.
➤ Perspective is one of the keys to peace and praise.
➤ I recommend writing out a gratitude list.

Refocus on confession and repentance.
➤ Confession is the first step to change. (Joshua 3:5)
➤ Repentance is the key to sustained change. (2 Corinthians 7:10-11)

➤ How do I truly repent?
  ▷ You must replace love of sin with hatred of sin.
  ▷ You must replace worldly sorrow with godly sorrow.
  ▷ You must confess and repent from the heart and not just the head.

➤ What are the results of repentance?
  The following results of repentance come from 2 Corinthians 7:10-11:
  ▷ You earnestly pursue righteousness.
  ▷ You regain the trust of others.
  ▷ You are angry over sin.
  ▷ You stand in awe of God.
  ▷ You repair relationships.
  ▷ You are passionate for God.
  ▷ You stand up for justice.
  ▷ You grow in holiness.

Refocus on accountability and encouragement.
➤ Friendships inspire faithfulness.
➤ Friendships help determine the direction and quality of your life.

1 Thessalonians 2:7-8
⁷But we proved to be gentle among you, as a nursing mother tenderly cares for her own children. ⁸Having so fond an affection for you, we were well-pleased to impart to you not only the gospel of God but also our own lives, because you had become very dear to us.

2 Timothy 2:1-2

[1]You therefore, my son, be strong in the grace that is in Christ Jesus. [2]The things which you have heard from me in the presence of many witnesses, entrust these to faithful men who will be able to teach others also.

➤ Everyone needs people to run the race with them. (Hebrews 12:1-3)
  ▷ Who is running the race ahead of you?
      Who is your Paul (your mentor)?
  ▷ Who is running the race beside you?
      Who is your Barnabas (your peer)?
  ▷ Who is running the race behind you?
      Who is your Timothy (your mentee)?

—— Appendix B ——
PRIORITY TIME EXAMPLE

Here's an example of a priority time that models the four principles of *Focused Thinking, Personal Application, Interactive Prayer* and *Life Journaling* for you to apply in your own times with God.

> **John 15:1-2**
> *"I am the true vine, and My Father is the vinedresser. Every branch in Me that does not bear fruit, He takes away; and every branch that bears fruit, He prunes it so that it may bear more fruit."*

FOCUSED THINKING
What does the vinedresser do?
"I am the true vine, and My Father is the vinedresser. Every branch in Me that does not bear fruit *He takes away*, and every branch that does bear fruit *He prunes*, that it may bear more fruit."

Who are the people in the story?
The vine is *Jesus*.
The vinedresser is *God the Father*.
The branches are *you and me*.

What is the vinedresser's job?
He is the *keeper* of the garden.
He *inspects* the branches for fruit.

What happens when the vinedresser doesn't see fruit?
He *takes away* – He lifts up and cleans.
- ➤ He cleans off the dust, mud and mildew.
- ➤ He wraps the vines around the trellis or ties them up.
- ➤ He doctors the branches.

What happens when the vinedresser sees fruit?
He *prunes* – He thins, reduces and cuts the vine.

Why does He prune the vine?
He prunes it so that it will bear *more fruit*.
- ➤ Pruning isn't fun, but it's necessary.
- ➤ Pruning is the key to having more.

PERSONAL APPLICATION

Where are you bearing fruit?
Where are you reaping a harvest? Be specific.
What did you sow to reap that harvest? Be specific.

What are your results?
Don't make this answer too complicated; fruit is obvious, you know it when you see it.

Where are you not bearing fruit?
Be honest.
Be specific.

How is God pruning you right now?
How is He pushing you toward *more fruit*?
How is He pushing you toward *much fruit*?

FOCUSED THINKING

John 15:3-5
"You are already clean because of the word which I have spoken to you. Abide in Me, and I in you. As the branch cannot bear fruit of itself unless it abides in the vine, so neither can you unless you abide in Me. I am the vine, you are the branches; he who abides in Me and I in him, he bears much fruit, for apart from Me you can do nothing."

What does the word "abide" mean?
To *remain* or to stay closely *connected*.

What can the branch *not* do by itself?
Bear fruit.

How does the branch bear fruit?
By *abiding* – by remaining and staying connected.
- ➤ You *worship God*.
- ➤ You *connect with friends*.
- ➤ You *invest in others*.

What are the results of abiding?
Bearing *fruit, more fruit* and *much fruit* (John 15:2, 5).

PERSONAL APPLICATION

Where are you bearing *fruit*?
Where are you bearing *more fruit?*
Where are you bearing *much fruit?*

It's this *simple!*
- ➤ YES to *Abiding* = YES to *Fruit*
- ➤ NO to *Abiding* = NO to *Fruit*

You don't bear fruit by only learning; you bear fruit by applying.
- ➤ There are no other options.
- ➤ You don't have to fully understand to be fully obedient.

The harvest won't be immediate; it will be in season.
- ➤ Sow now, reap later.
- ➤ Sow long enough to reap later.

You don't bear fruit in *every season*; you bear fruit *in season*.

Where do you need to *work harder* at *abiding* (staying closely connected)?

INTERACTIVE PRAYER

Father, search my heart and show me the specific ways I can abide in You more. Forgive me for the ways I'm too busy for the abiding relationship. Father, never let me get too comfortable in my abiding relationship with You. I pray for You to keep pushing me to bear fruit, more fruit and much fruit. Give me the ability to persevere through challenges and crises. Give me the ability to receive your pruning with the right attitude. I pray for You to prune me in my physical health. Give me the desire, discipline and determination to exercise and diet daily. I pray for You to prune me in my schedule. Give me the ability to honor my priorities. Forgive me for working too much. Help me to say YES to my major priorities so that I will say NO to my minor priorities.
I pray for You to discipline my children for their good so they

may share in Your holiness. I pray for You to prune my children so that they will glorify You by bearing much fruit. I pray for You to prove to my children the importance of staying closely connected to You. Show them that apart from You they can do nothing. Give them Your perspective on life and Your sense of urgency in regards to time. I pray for You to bless Karin's abiding and give her the privilege of bearing much fruit as a wife, mother, leader and teacher. I pray for her life and ministry to glorify You by bearing much fruit.

I pray for Christ-followers to never be content with average. I pray for You to give them a vision for abiding and the abundance that comes from abiding. I pray for them to abide by drawing near to You, holding fast to You, stimulating one another to love and good deeds, and encouraging one another. I pray for them to bear much fruit by worshiping You, connecting with friends and investing in others. I pray for You to give them a vision for the abundance of revival. I pray for our people to repent of not abiding. I pray for them to repent of being satisfied with anything less than much fruit. I pray for our people to desire to glorify You by bearing much fruit and proving to be Your disciples.

LIFE JOURNALING

Everything you've just read is my process of life journaling. I use this space to journal where I'm at personally in life so that these truths are placed in the proper context and timing of what's going on in and around me. I also use this space to journal what's happening in the lives of my wife, kids and ministry. For example, the fact that I am the father of two high school students is definitely creating a sense of urgency as I think about this subject of abiding and abundance in their lives. I want them to experience what it's like to bear much fruit and to glorify God before they go to college because I want them to have a vision for living a better story. As of today, Mark only has 86 weeks until graduation and Annika only has 138 weeks. What needs to happen in the next 100 weeks for them to learn the true value of abiding in Christ before college?

NOTES

1. Baker, John. *Celebrate Recovery*. Grand Rapids, MI: Zondervan, 1998.

2. Hendricks, Howard G. and William D. Hendricks. *Living by the Book*. Chicago: Moody Press, 1991.

3. Miller, John G. *QBQ! The Question Behind the Question*. New York: G.P. Putnam's Sons, 2004.

4. Willard, Dallas. *The Great Omission: Reclaiming Jesus' Essential Teachings on Discipleship.* San Fransico: Harper Collins, 2006.

5. Rath, Tom. *StrengthsFinder.* New York: Gallup Press, 2007.

ABOUT CHRIS

A native of Memphis, TN, Chris Conlee has responded to God's call to impact his hometown. In the midst of his collegiate golf career, Chris had a crisis of belief that led him to abandon his dream of golf and to relentlessly pursue the heart of God. After completing his Bachelor's Degree from the University of Memphis and his Master of Divinity from Mid-America Baptist Theological Seminary, Chris followed God's direction to plant a church that would be a perfect place for imperfect people.

In 2002 Highpoint, a non-denominational church, became that place. Chris's conviction to create an environment of compassion without compromise allows the dechurched, unchurched and churched of the Mid-South to have a God-centered, relevant church home.

With a heart for people and the ability to cast vision, Chris has used his leadership and teaching strengths in both the church and business community. As Highpoint Church has grown to thousands of people in multiple locations, the *Memphis Business Journal* named Chris one of the "Top 40 Under 40" leaders in the city.

Chris is married to his best friend Karin and they have two children, Mark and Annika. Chris loves to spend his free time taking his wife out on dates, watching his children play sports, reading leadership books and autobiographies, and cheering on the Memphis Tigers basketball team.

You can learn more about Chris and his ministry at highpointmemphis.com, and you can follow him on twitter (@chrisconlee) and on Facebook (/chris.conlee.54).

Made in the USA
Lexington, KY
15 August 2014